EL'AZAR; YESHU;

AND

TMA

EL'AZAR; YESHU;

AND

TMA

{MORE OR LESS A NOVEL}

JOHN MCGINLEY

iUniverse®

EL'AZAR; YESHU; AND TMA
{MORE OR LESS A NOVEL}

iUniverse books may be ordered through booksellers or by contacting:

iUniverse
1663 Liberty Drive
Bloomington, IN 47403
www.iuniverse.com
1-800-Authors (1-800-288-4677)

ISBN: 978-1-4917-9269-8 (sc)
ISBN: 978-1-4917-9268-1 (hc)
ISBN: 978-1-4917-9251-3 (e)

Print information available on the last page.

iUniverse rev. date: 03/11/2016

DEDICATION.

With love and admiration I dedicate this book to:

MEGHAN McGINLEY HELMS

A BEAUTIFUL WOMAN
A BEAUTIFUL MOTHER
A BEAUTIFUL DAUGHTER
and:

A BEAUTIFUL SALARY!

Avis:

To my dear and cherished reader <that is, if there are any>:

I myself never kept a diary. My sense of a diary is to the effect that the given entries of a diarist are often repetitious; but not literally repetitious. In this production each and every repetitious entry is a repetitious expansion; and/or correction of an expression; and/or an adjustment.

I am -- more or less – writing as a diarist. Not necessarily a strict diary of the days and weeks of my life. Rather, a 'diary' of the days and weeks, and months of this production. I am not aiming for the Nobel Prize in Literature. *I am simply writing the only way I can now write at all. If such is a deficiency, then so be it.*

***** ***** *****

PROLOG-A

Those clever Rabbis at the twilight time of the closing of the Talmud *Bavli* chose satire as a way of: i). making the point, and, at the same time, ii). making the point without ruffling the caveats of Rabbinic Officialdom. Listen to this clever --- but weighty ---- story. It is a satire with regard to an ever-growing proliferation (i.e., like cancer) of Oral Torah *halakhot* and Rabbinic Enactments and, as well, a germane satire on the figure of Rabbi Aqiba. To wit:

When Moses ascended to the (Heavenly) ***Heights he found the Holy One, blessed be He, as He was sitting and attaching crowns to some of the letters*** (and adding *tagin* to certain letters). ***Moses said to His face:* "Who is holding you back** (from giving the Torah as it is)***? Hashem replied to***

him: "There is a man who is destined to exist at the end of many generations ------- Aqiba ben Yosef is his name; he will expound upon each and every matter HEAPS UPON HEAPS OF *HALAKHOT*."

Moses addressed the face of Hashem: "Master of the Universe, show him to me!" *Hashem said to him:* "Turn around" (he, <Moses> found himself in Aqiba's class). ***Moses went and sat at the end of eight rows of students. But he*** (Moses <who received the Law from Sinai) ***did not understand what they were saying. Moses' strength ebbed. Once they reached a certain matter which was puzzling. Aqiba's students asked him:*** "from what source do you know this? *Aqiba replied* (cavalierly): "It is a *halakha* transmitted from the mouth of Moses at Sinai."

Moses' mind was relieved. He returned and came before the Holy One, blessed be He. Moses said to His face:

"YOU HAVE SOMEONE LIKE THIS AND YOU GIVE THE TORAH TRHOUGH ME!!??"

Hashem said to him: "SHUSH! Thus has it arisen in the thoughts before Me."

Moses said to His face:

"Master of the Universe, You have shown me his Torah; now show me his reward."

"TURN AROUND."

Moses turned around and saw that the people were weighing the flesh from [Aqiba's body] *in the meat market.*

Moses said before Hashem:

"MASTER OF THE UNIVERSE!!! Such is his Torah and THIS is reward???

Hashem replied:

"QUIET!!!! SUCH IS MY DECREE.

***** ***** *****

Again, our *Bavli* is, often enough, construed to be speak by indirection with regard to how It can get a point sustained without arousing the hackles of Rabbinic Officialdom. The most salient point of the passage is the revelation of Rabbi Aqiba's fondness of multiplying *halakhot*:

"There is one man who is destined to exist at the end of many generations; Aqiba ben Yosef is his name: he will expound each and every matter; *HEAPS UPON HEAPS OF* HALAKHOT."

{*Bavli* Gemara on Tractate *Menahot* as, roughly, per 29b-i --- 30b-ii <Art Scroll>

****

****

****

PROLOG-B

SHUVU!

SHUVU!

OH WAYWARD CHILDREN

Jeremiah 3:14

*****

SHUVU!

SHUVU!

OH WAYWARD CHILDREN

{rha-m stooh}

{Hoot-s* *m-Ahr*}

*. There is, in both English <"except"> and Hebrew <"hoot-s"> an ambiguity present in these two words; that is to say that both "except" and "hoot-s" share an ambiguity. "EXCEPT" and

"Hoot-s" in both languages can be deployed in opposite manners. The "except" of English and the "hoot-s" of Hebrew are symmetrically ambiguous insofar as both the English preposition and the Hebrew preposition can be deployed as opposites. Generally speaking, in both languages and with both words, the "privation" meaning dominates. That having been stipulated, it still remains the case that both words, in context, can connote fulfillment as well.

With both words ----- "EXCePT" and "HooT-s" -- the context of the sentence determines, in both cases, the valid meaning. In both languages the prepositions <"HooT-s"> and <"EXCePT"> each symmetrically allow for opposite meanings, again leaving it to the context to determine the meaning of the given sentence.
Consider the following:

Everyone in the graduation ceremony ***except*** *John received their diplomas on graduation night. It turns out that John had failed the Greek exam thus not qualifying for graduation.*

In this case the "except" (aka "*hoot-s*") is deployed as a privation.
Then there is this:

Everyone in the graduation ceremony ***except*** *Miriam received their diplomas on graduation night*
Miriam did not receive her diploma with her class. She finished all the requirements for graduation by the end of her third year of high-school and thereby qualified to start her college career earlier by one year.

In this case, the "except" (aka "*hoot-s*") is deployed as a fulfillment.

What is the point?
There are sections in our Talmud *Bavli* wherein our final anonymous editors were able to "fly under the radar" in making subtle insertions into the final editing of the full text. We have, herewith, one of those subtle insertions:

SHUVU

SHUVU!

OH WAYWARD CHILDREN

{rha-m stooh}

{Hoot-S m-Ahr}*

In this case these crafty final anonymous editors trade on this ambiguity cited just above. Surfacely the *hoo*t-s functions in the mode of privation: *AHER* is excluded from "returning." The "wayward children" were not saints; they were wayward. But they still could "return." On the other hand the putative natural sense of the verse from *Jeremiah* 3:14 it appears that *AHER* was SO wicked that he would be excluded from *Jeremiah*'s urgent plea. HOWEVER: The phrasing in our *Hagigah* Gemara is subtle. *Hoot-s* ---- as with "except" ---- has an opposite meaning. "The wayward children" phrase retains its meaning, but in a radically paradoxical way. The opposite meaning of "except"/'*hoo*t-S' turns the semantic meaning of *Jeremiah*'s call in an un-expected manner. Yes; the word "un-expected" here seems to be out-of-place. Yet the phrasing does in fact, and validly, **allows** for the unexpected meaning.
To wit: *Aher* does not fall under the caveat of *Jeremiah's* plea. How so?

Aher does not have to "return" for *Aher* ***NEVER LEFT!****

In this matter the final anonymous editors <see below> slip in (and under the radar, so to speak) a momentous and unexpected teaching. What was the momentous and unexpected teaching? It should be clear: Scripture-centricity was for Judaism the *status quo ante*. This was upended with the Pharisaic invention of the Oral Torah. Worse than that, that invention <and its accoutrements> tended <albeit never "officially"> to be honored even over the *mitsvot* of Scripture. Such was a crime from <u>*within*</u> *Beit Yisrael* and it has not been overturned; on the contrary.

*****

Throughout the centuries by which our Talmud *Bavli* came to be completed there came to be -- towards the closing of the Talmud *Bavli* a group of scholars active roughly from 575ce through 610ce -- who came to be known as "The Final Anonymous Editors." Their open and widely known mandate was to produce a literary production worthy of the seriousness of the great endeavor. The "Palestinian Talmud" -- a shorter endeavor -- was weak on many levels. The mandate of the group (here we are speaking of the Talmud *Bavli*) -- which came to be referred to as "the Final Anonymous Editors" -- was to produce a much more accurate production along with literary finesse which was so lacking in the Palestinian Talmud.

Obviously there were many opportunities, then, to go beyond their mandate.

In contrast, Rabbinic Officialdom, throughout the centuries by which this great Talmud *Bavli* achievement was to be completed, often interjected themselves into the emergence of prior sections of the *Gemarot* of this HUGE production so as to be in sync with a certain orientation favored by "Rabbinic Officialdom": i.e., keeping things *kosher*: <<"*kosher*" in this Rabbinic/Pharasaic frame of reference means that the "ORAL TORAH" is validated ------((and, further, the case can be easily made that in practice <albeit not officially> "Rabbinic Officialdom" *de facto* honors the *halakhot* of the Oral Torah more than it honors the *mitsvot* of Scripture))>>.

*****

In any case, the emergence of that subtle coterie called "The Final Anonymous Editors" somehow gained a great deal of autonomy as to the final editing of the Talmud *Bavli*. This grouping <from circa 575----610> was very much influenced by the early figures at Yavne **prior** to the *Putsch* (of 93/93ce) which put the Pharisaic faction* in control of the Yavne Community.

*****

To be sure the Pharisaic Sect was dominant in Rabbinic affairs. Over time the Rabbinic Movement dropped the nomenclature of "The Pharisees" in favor of "The Rabbis" since most Rabbis were largely in synch with the goals and deployments of what used to be called "The Pharisees." Indeed, for better or for worse, the spirit (((and worse ESPECIALLY with respect to their romance with the Oral Torah))) of the Rabbinic Movement (even unto the Modern Age) was rather Pharisaic in its orientation.

But there was also, thank Heaven, that offsetting grouping. A grouping which would culminate in that grouping above: "The Final Anonymous Editors" of the Talmud *Bavli*.

The offsetting grouping was the child of a chain -- started by Rabbi Meir* when he went "East" -- of subtle Rabbis over these intervening centuries and which coalesced into "The Final Anonymous Editors." The group of which we are now speaking -- "The Final Anonymous

Editors" -- quietly and with subtlety advanced a counter *ethos* into the Talmud *BAVLI* which harkened back to the Scripture-centric (and only Scripture-centric) orientation of the first two decades of the Yavne Community. {The figures of this "chain" have been reviewed in detail in my "Jerusalem/Athens Production.}
What made all this possible were giants in each generation -- actually hearkening back to Rebbe/ Rabbi himself -- who quietly allowed the *sub rosa* figures in each generation to maintain a *sub rosa* underground which animated the hope of a RETURN/**SHUVU!** to the Scripture-centric orientation. The figures who became the "final anonymous editors" managed to gain enough power such that their autonomy in the service of generating a good literary product for the Talmud *Bavli* actually spilled over to a kind of a subterranean *ethos* -- from generation unto generation -- which kept ((and even posterior to the time of the 'final anonymous editors')) and keeps, without nomenclature, the hope to a RETURN/ **SHUVU**! to the orientation of the founding fathers of the Yavne Community.
****
****

Ellie Wiesel's Meditation:

Man was created not to know happiness but truth. To discover it, one must start anew; everything must be reviewed. Man, chosen by God, must chose Him in turn. All ready-made answers, all seemingly unalterable certainties serve only to provide a good conscience to those who like to sleep and live peaceably. To avoid spending a lifetime tracking down truth, one pretends to have found it. But -- so one says in Kotzk -- ***Revelation Itself,*** *once it has become a habit and a front, becomes suspect.*

[Wiesel, 1972. Page 241.]
****

Truth is the Seal of Hashem and it is our duty to be true, so to speak, to Truth. The history of Christianity -- with only few and far between exceptions -- has a horrible history of overt and endemic Anti-Semitism. I have not shied away from this terrible Truth in the writing of this book (and also in my prior productions).

But there is another Truth which has arisen roughly from the run-up to the Holocaust on up to the present day. Most Christians played it safe during those dark years. But a fair amount of Christians rose to the occasion to help -- even to the cost of their own lives -- to save Jews, especially the children.

In more recent times -- and on the global scene -- Christians have become second only to Jews in supporting the Nation of Israel and the People of Israel. In an undertaking such as this production it would be sinful on my part to recognize only the <<OUTRAGEOUSLY CRUEL>> past while ignoring the present. Jews in general and Jews in the Nation of Israel are being supported in various ways by Christians, who, in doing such, are acting AS Christians. It is heart-warming. Indeed I can think of no other grouping than Christians which, on the whole, has steadfastly* been supportive to Jews from the time of the Holocaust and supportive as well of the Nation of Israel.

*. (Steadfastly???? Only recently.
Even as one celebrates this support by Christians of and for *Beit Yisrael* in our time one must never forget the outrageously sinful, **over many centuries**, treatment by Christians relative to Judaism as a whole

and the hateful *programs* visited upon Jews (((think especially of the children))) ***for many, many centuries***. It remains an ugly heritage with the support of the Papacy over many centuries.)

****
****

Rabbi Aqiba had been mentored by that quirkish Gam-zu. Later on it would be Rabbi Joshua <Aqiba's second mentor> who introduced Aqiba to the Rabbi who would be the mentor of both: El'azar ben Hurcanus; later, simply 'Rabbi El'azar.'
JWM 7/27/14

****
****
****
****
****
****

<u>PART ONE.</u>

There are a number of Rabbis noted in the *Mishna* and the *Bavli* who have the name "Rabbi El'azar." The "Rabbi El'azar" of which we speak is an amazing figure. Let me count the ways:
i). He is the young adolescent who hailed from Bethany, say, circa no earlier than 29ce and no later than 33ce. He was the young son in a wealthy estate in Bethany who came under the suasion of Yeshu. His father took notice of this and made inquiries about this curious figure named Yehoshua. Unlike most, this figure <Yehoshua aka Yeshu> did not trade on his family name and for good reason <i.e., scandal>. Yes, his name was "Yehoshua" but from the time of HIS adolescence he was referred to as "Yeshu." It stuck for the rest of his life.

ii). The young El'azar continued to show up whenever "The Preacher" preached. Yeshu came to know that this young man hailed from a very wealthy and influential family.
iii). The father made it his business to investigate this odd figure who, clearly, had become under the Preacher's persuasion.

The feedback received by El'azar's father included interesting features about this Preacher. The negative first of all: this Yeshu was a *mamzer*. This did not sit well with the father. On the other hand, this curious figure was well--trained in Scripture. More than that this Preacher had a knack to reveal that Scripture was alive; so alive that it could change a person's whole orientation of one's life. The father warmed up to this preacher.
iv). There was a downside. The Preacher did not accept the Pharasaic invention of the "Oral Torah." Indeed this Preacher rudely ridiculed the "Oral Torah" contention. The family in Bethany were all Pharasaically oriented. Nonetheless El'azar's father wanted to know more about this Preacher.
v). The Preacher was, in turn, fascinated with this wealthy family. El'azar's father allowed El'azar to spend time with him alone as they probed "The Law and the Prophets." [[The third and final Section of Scripture had not yet been finished; indeed it would be about thirty-five years before the Canon would be closed.]]
vi). All of this -- from both sides -- turned out to be a rising crescendo. The father -- by way of his son -- suggested that the Preacher come to the Bethany Estate for dinner and an overnight visit.
It was very successful for all parties. The father still was concerned with the Preacher's attitude toward the Oral Torah orientation. On the other hand there was no downplaying the change in the

youngish El'azar; he probed Scripture and became well educated in Scripture.

vii). There were two older sisters in the household. Martha was the oldest. She was a very "down-to-earth" kind of person. She very quickly sized up Yeshu as someone who sooner or later would cause much *tsuris* (and, as it worked out, she was a prophetess). She avoided him. In contrast, the younger sister, Miriam, (who lavished affection upon her younger brother) became enthused with the often-charming Preacher. And Yeshu reciprocated.

*****

We shall talk about the fraud Resurrection scheme (((involving a Plan hatched by the High Priest Caiaphas with Yeshu and El'azar and even cleared by Pilate))) and how, in the final analysis, it blew up along with the HUGE after-effects of such a fraud. The effect of this fraud Resurrection had a radically adverse reaction upon Miriam. Miriam, most of all, was most devastated and falling to pieces for she ***experienced*** the death of her beloved brother only to find out that it was a sham. It was clear to all that this one/two punch to her sanity was something that she would never get over. She was never the same again.

This development -- Yeshu was very close with Miriam -- changed Yeshu completely. He broke down in tears; he could hardly save his breath. He was disgusted with himself. For the first time in his life he looked inward; and he didn't like what he saw. He wanted to die. But he wanted to die in such a way that at least El'azar would not be the center of the blame for this outrageous fraud. He counselled El'azar to stay out of the picture as much as he could. El'azar was confused by what was happening; but he followed Yeshu's advice.

*****

There were no secrets in that 'backwater' settlement called Nazareth. As a very young adolescent Yeshu came to know that he was a *mamzer*. He carried this shame for the rest of his life. He came to know who his true father was: The Sidonian Archer who was drafted into the Roman Army. Rather handsome. As an archer this soldier could choose any household in virtually any town or city for the night or nights of bivouac. When his contingent bivouacked in Nazareth he was drawn to the home of the "Hair Dresser." That night Yeshu was conceived.

Again, there were no secrets in that backwater town. Everyone -- eventually including Yeshu -- came to know who the father was. The missing father was very much on his mind both in his childhood and as a grown man. His next two siblings were conceived and reared by Yosef, a relative who lived in Bethlehem, and who came up to Nazareth to be a husband to Miriam. After Yosef died, his brother took over and produced with the "Hair Dresser" two more boys and one girl. All of ***them*** had a father who lived under the same roof. Not so for Yeshu.

He chased the Sidonian Archer but never came into contract with him.

There were, then, two deep and difficult matters weighing on this adolescent. The Missing Father; AND, the deep embarrassment of a Mother known as a 'Hair-Dresser.' One way or another these deep and difficult matters stayed with him in one form or another.

***** ***** *****

Let's get something out of the way.

This El'azar is the same person who, in the Talmud *Bavli*, was referred to as "Rabbi Eliezer" (ben Hurcanus).

*****

It is widely known that the Christian enemies of Judaism would cull the *Bavli* for (putative) slurs against Christianity in general and against Yeshu in particular. These putative slurs (they were true-but-dangerous for Judaism). *Beit Yisrael* in this time period, for all practical purposes, was a People-without-a-country by virtue of that ill-conceived *Bar Kochba* Revolt followed by the hateful Hadrianic Repression. A People-without-a-country is a People in a constant dangerous situation. These putative "slurs" were simply facts; facts which made Christian Officialdom uneasy and willing to kill Jews and/or burn their sacred manuscripts (the *Bavli* most especially <both as it was being created and then, later, as a finished product>).

The Jewish reaction was to blur some of the nomenclature for certain figures who were salient in the text of the *Bavli*.

The figure <long dead before the Talmud *Bavli* was inaugurated> which is being presented in this endeavor is Rabbi El'azar who hailed from Bethany and, as an adolescent, was the one closest to Yeshu. This figure had an amazing set of experiences while Yeshu was alive and, many years after Yeshu's crucifixion, another set of experiences <having nothing to do with his relationship with Yeshu> as a star at the *Beit ha-Midrash* of the Yavne Community to which we shall attend below.

> Let us cut to the chase: This remarkable figure <i.e., El'azar ben Hurcanus> loomed large during Yeshu's ministry. This remarkable figure -- post crucifixion -- also spent some time in the "min" which was known as 'The Jerusalem Community' headed by Jacob* who was the second child of that Nazareth family <albeit with a different father> and the one who was closest to Yeshu, both growing up and afterwards as well. Jacob, however, stayed in Nazareth after Yeshu left the homestead in Nazareth. Later, when Jacob heard about the emerging denouement of what was going on between the ridiculous false "resurrection" and its somber aftermath from one of Yeshu's other half-brothers ((his name was Yehuda and a follower of Yeshu)) he, Jacob, high-tailed down (actually "up") to Jerusalem. He arrived just after the demise of Yeshu.

***** ***** ***** ***** *****

The Empty Tomb.

There were two half-brothers of Yeshu in that "rag-tag" set of disciples who followed Yeshu: Yehuda and Shimon <<but not the Shimon who was known as "The Rock">>. They were shocked and somewhat disgusted with what Yeshu did at Bethany. They too knew how this whole fraudulent farce affected Miriam (the younger sister of Martha and the sister of El'azar). She was falling apart. Yeshu himself would not respond to Yehuda and Shimon's overtures for ironing things out. And both of them -- Yehuda and Shimon -- had the sense that Yeshu was taking a turn towards self-destruction. The only person who could speak to Yeshu on an equal footing with Yeshu was his half-brother, Jacob, who was less than a year younger than Yeshu and who was very close to his slightly older half-brother. Prior to his decision to be a Preacher he would -- back in Nazareth -- come back to Jacob when he, Yeshu, was in a depressed mood. <<This was a common problem with Yeshu.>> But now Jacob was in Nazareth and Yeshu was in Jerusalem.

Yehuda, the Treasurer of the rag-tag Group, used the money to hire out two horses so that they could get to Jacob and get Jacob to come down from Nazareth with them as soon as possible. When they reached Nazareth they were welcomed warmly. Jacob had missed them dearly. The two half-brothers, Yehuda and Shimon, told him about the hoax; about Miriam's irreversible Breakdown; and the uncanny -- perhaps even self-destructive -- mood which had come over Yeshu after Miriam's experience.
Jacob was not surprised by any of this. He knew Yeshu better than Yeshu knew himself. He shed tears for what he, Jacob, presumed his half-brother was going through. He agreed with Yehuda and Shimon that it was possible that Yeshu would deal with this horrible imbroglio with what today would be called manic and depressive shields. Jacob told the two that it was incumbent that they -- including himself -- go down ("up" in another sense) to Jerusalem as soon as possible. Without explaining, Jacob rolled out his cart from the shed and had the horses pull all three of them back to Jerusalem. Jacob didn't have to explain; all of them KNEW at some level, that they would not see Yeshu alive ever again.

When they arrived Jacob went straight to the layout of Caiaphas' rather luxorious land and home. Jacob had never met him. But he knew that Caiaphas was the key figure for getting the body back to the family for a proper burial. If you or I; or for that matter Yehuda and Shimon -------------- we would all have been escorted, rudely, off the premises. But Jacob had a quiet but commanding demeanor about him. The guards went back to Caiaphas and all three were welcomed into his somewhat lavish quarters.

Caiaphas revealed to them that this very moment Yeshu was being cut down from the Roman Cross. A friend of Caiaphas who admired Yeshu from a distance had offered his own tomb for Yeshu's remains.

For the three half-brothers of Yeshu (but brothers to each other) it sank in. It was one thing to ride on a cart absent the dead body. But from this time forward it would the moment of truth.

Caiaphas had made the appropriate orders about the guards who were assigned to the tomb since it was not clear at all that some sort of hanky-panky might occur {{{after all it was just shy of a week wherein there was HUGE hanky-panky about two miles down the road: Bethany. There was resurrection fever in Jerusalem as *Pesach* was falling on Shabbat}}}. After all, "resurrection" -- one way or another -- was still in the air. Caiaphas made it his business that there simply would be none of that "resurrection" mania.

Yes. Already the "Great *Shabbat*" had started. But Caiaphas understood that what the brothers had to do trumped the *Halakha* in this matter. By eleven o-clock the three brothers loaded Yeshu's scared and wounded corpse onto the cart. Yehuda and Shimon opted to stay in Jerusalem and promised that they would come back to Nazareth in the near future.

The three brothers and Caiaphas chatted for a bit. Yehuda and Shimon took their leave. Jacob, then, decided that he would get on the road back to Nazareth. But Caiaphas persuaded Jacob to deal with what he, Caiaphas, deemed was a delicate, AND VERY IMPORTANT, matter. Tired as he was, Jacob nevertheless agreed to stay longer. And he did.

*****

Or this way:

As we have seen, Jacob had demanded an audience from the High Priest and received such at once. Caiaphas and Jacob had a long discussion. Jacob made it clear that the body would be brought back to the homestead at Nazareth for final burial. Caiaphas agreed; he suggested that the corpse be removed from the temporary burial site in Jerusalem with the understanding that the corpse would be interred back at the homestead in Nazareth. Indeed, doing such, lightened the load for Caiaphas.

They -- Caiaphas and Jacob -- agreed that If some of Yeshu's followers drummed up **YET ANOTHER FALSE RESSURECTON** then so be it. Truth often hides itself.

Accordingly, as Friday evening was becoming early Saturday morning <<<in darkness of course>>>, the corpse was removed; and Jacob returned with the body. The requisites according to this very private endeavor would go against the *Halakha*. Caiaphas made it clear that under the circumstances ((the removal of the body which would be brought to the homestead in Nazareth in the dark of night)) the *Halakha* of the situation was, *de facto*, suspended.

Caiaphas had been very impressed by Jacob. Yeshu was mercurial; one would never know for sure what his next "enterprise" would be. In contrast, this Jacob half-brother had his feet on the ground. Yes he also dabbled in the "magical" arts from time to time; but not nearly the way Yeshu did. By and large, this Jacob was solid. One could trust this man. And, indeed, Caiaphas, as we shall see, persuaded Jacob to (((when the burial at Nazareth was accomplished along with the requisites -- some of time -- were accomplished))) take on the mantle of the position which, according to the original contours of "The Plan" which would have fallen to Yeshu.

[[[Speaking of character traits there is this: With age our much older El'azar could react in a mercurial manner as well, especially when his colleagues at Yavne would (-- more by indirection than straight-out --) bring up his close relationship with Yeshu as well as his time with Jacob who ended up running the *min* referred to as "The Jerusalem Community."]]]

****
****
****
****

About two weeks later, Caiaphas brought up "The Plan" to Jacob and how it was sabotaged by the dramatic and searing aftermath of that false

Resurrection in Bethany. Jacob was surprised that "the Plan" would have entailed that Yeshu would have become the High Priest <<<and ordained so as to articulate aloud the true Sacred NAME in the Holy of Holies in the Temple!!!!!>>> for the poor and disenfranchised.
But reflection made one realize that the whole situation in Jerusalem was at a crisis.
The Roman Occupation was breaking the spirit of the Jewish population. The Roman Occupation also generated many young Jewish males to be willing to set in motion a Rebellion against the horrific Occupation. These were the stupid ones and Caiaphas had been hoping that "The Plan" could siphon off the dangerously growing population who wanted to Revolt against Rome which anyone with any brains knew would be an horrific blood-bath and, possibly, the end of *Yisrael* as a country. Caiaphas understood that there is a huge difference between having a country under a horrible "Occupation" in contrast to losing the country entirely.*
Then Caiaphas dropped a bomb on Jacob. Caiaphas now wanted this half-brother of Yeshu to hold the office of the High Priest for the disenfranchised and the poor. In the original plan such was to accrue to Yeshu. But all of that blew-up as the fraud Resurrection brought about chaos: unintended consequences.
Holding that office, as we have seen, entailed (among many other lesser functions) that the High Priest would enter into the "Holy of Holies" and articulate the True Name from *Exodus* 3:14. <<<<The four letter name in of 3:15 was but a close circumlocution of the True NAME in 3:14.>>>>
Jacob was stunned. He also felt that he was not worthy of such (as opposed to Yeshu who -- when

alerted to what Caiaphas had in his plan -- had quickly accepted with no qualms).

*. Of course such is exactly what would happen about a century later. The turning point was when Rabbi Aqiba orchestrated a bit of wickedness by, in effect, ratcheting this whole thing into a Rebellion against Rome. Aqiba was deeply infatuated with that corrupt "Son of a Star" who was already pushing for Rebellion. Rabbi Aqiba -- most unfortunately -- managed to put the High Estimation of the Rabbinic Movement behind this jerk-off who called himself "Son of a Star." At this time of Jewish history (post Temple) the Rabbinate was the institution which kept *Beit Yisrael* from falling apart. It was highly honored. Many Jews counselled that it would be FOOLISH to take on the Romans. But Rabbi Aqiba persuaded a majority of the Rabbinate to "liberate" themselves by supporting the barely educated "Son of a Star." [More like, a SOB]
*****
We all know about Hadrian. The Revolt failed; failed with rivers of Jewish Blood. Of all the military disasters in the history of *Beit Yisrael* this was the most stupid. Rivers of Jewish Blood. But there was something even worse.
Hadrian decided to effectuate the end of Jewish Polity **at all** for *Erets Yisrael*. This "Bar Kochba Revolt" -- followed by the horrendous Hadrianic Repression -- effectively ended Jewish Polity of their own Land. This was the beginning of the decisive Exile of Judaism as a Nation.

Yes. It is true that *Erets Yisrael* always had SOME Jews (but mostly sparse) in the Land of Israel. But there was no Jewish Polity. This -- the *Bar Kochba* Revolt followed by the horror of the Hadrianic Repression -- was the beginning of the Jewish Diaspora. It would last for roughly eighteen centuries.

****
****

We were speaking of El'azar. More to the point we were speaking of El'azar AS "Rabbi Eliezer."
Below we shall follow some further developments in El'azar's life prior to his admission into the Yavne Community. In any case this "Rabbi Eliezer <ben Hurcanus>" came to be a HUGE player in the Yavne Community.
But we are getting ahead of ourselves. At this point <roughly 33ce> we must remember that there was no Yavne in existence or even a plan to have a Yavne. Nonetheless, we must now engage the matter of the true phonetic of El'azar's name. As pointed out above the writers of the Talmud *Bavli* made a decision to transform *orally* El'azar (ben Hurcanus) to "Eliezer." Phonetically such is a substantial change. But in written form there really is no difference. The writers of the Talmud *Bavli* simply "marked" the mute Hebrew vowels differently from the way "El'azar" had properly been marked. Without really changing the letters themselves (mute or not mute) the marking of the mute vowels <as *per* "El'azar"> could come forth orally quite different from the way the mute vowels were marked to come forth audibly allowing for "Eliezer." It's that simple. And over the centuries most non-Jews <and even many Jews> counted "Eliezer" as a different name fully different from "El'azar."

And what's the point?
One point should be obvious from the beginning. "El'azar" hearkens the Christian "Lazarus." The writers of the Talmud *Bavli* did not want the great JEWISH figure who was the greatest of all halakhists to be associated with the nomenclature "El'azar/Lazarus"; a nomenclature which would call to mind "Yeshu." It would only fuzz up the demarcation of what is Jewish and what is Christian. And never forget the following in this vein: To be sure, the interaction among El'azar; Yeshu; El'azar's father; and of both Miriam and Martha **was quintessentially JEWISH** <albeit one would never guess such if one only read the putative "New Testament">.
*****
With the passage of time early Christianity tended to co-up this JEWISH affair as something which has little to do with Judaism and MUCH MORE to do with early Christianity. A concrete indication of all this is the radically **REVISED** version of Yeshu and "Lazarus" and Lazarus' family as *per* "The New Testament." Check it out for yourself unless you are fearful of getting conTAMinated in the process.
The other point is this:
The true reality of this whole imbroglio is this: ALL the players in this situation, involving Yeshu and El'azar, were born as Jews; lived as Jews; died as Jews. Period.
****
"This and That";
i). The Fourth Gospel* has the Thursday Night meal * as a putative "Yochanan" seated next to Yeshu. This putative "Yochanan" <as per the Fourth Gospel> was said to be "the Beloved Disciple."
By the time of the final redaction of this Fourth Gospel << -- it was the last of all the fully redacted Gospels -- >> the emergent Christian religion

(((which by this time was awash with Pauline** tropes most of which were **not at all** in synch with the *de facto* offerings of Yeshu))) was attempting to significantly distance Itself from the tropisms of Judaism.

Accordingly, the emerging 'Church' (((which by now had come to realize that "Lazarus/El'azar" emigrated back to his roots and was solidly back in the Jewish fold; indeed, he was the greatest *halakhist* in the Yavne Community))) re-named "El'azar" as "Yochanan." In fact there was no "Yochanan" at the Last Supper and, in fact, there was no significant follower of Yeshu named "Yochanan." The reality is that at the "last Supper" it was El'azar who was "the beloved disciple." But, over time, the nascent Christian religion did not want the closest disciple of Yeshu to be named "El'azar" since this figure <also referred to as "Rabbi Eliezer" (as we have seen above)> turned out to be a major player -- <u>and solidly Jewish</u> -- at Yavne. In other words the emerging Church did not desire at all SUCH a huge figure in Judaism to be the same figure who, in his adolescence, was mesmerized by Yeshu. After all, with the passage of time, our El'azar (aka "Rabbi Eliezer") came to eschew emergent Christianity totally and to eschew as well the created <created by the early Christian leaders> figure of a "Lazarus" put forth by the major figures of the Church in the early decades of Christianity.*

*. [This imbroglio raised its ugly head during the upheaval at Yavne circa 93/94 ce. The Pharasaic Sect at Yavne (-- it was a majority but a majority without <that is, yet> power --) took matters into their own hands led by Rabbis Joshua and Aqiba. With thuggish tactics, this Sect took total

control of the Yavne Community. And the first order of business was to maintain that the Oral Torah of the Pharisaic Sect should be incorporated into the determining of the *Halakha*.]*

**. {Prior to this Pharisaic *Coup* the Yavne Community was guided by Scripture-centricity *and only Scripture-centricity*. How this ugly change came to be has been reviewed in great detail in my prior productions and also in the production at hand.}

****

In the context of the Fourth Gospel El'azar was simply referred to as "the other disciple" by the Christian-oriented writers <with, later, the understanding that in certain influential Christian circles the manufactured nomenclature became "John"/"Yochanan">. Two names came to emerge for the one individual. "El'azar" was always the true name of the figure <the beloved disciple> involved whether of one is speaking of this figure in his youth and mesmerized by Yeshu: and/or that same figure who returned to a solid Jewish and only Jewish figure who was the greatest *halakhist* at Yavne>.

So, by rights, this "Beloved Disciple" should be allowed to be **called** "El'azar." But In documents ((this would mean the Talmud)) wherein there were marked Hebrew <and Aramaic> vowels, the name "El'azar" comes forth as 'Eliezer' (ben Hurcanas). The redactors of the Talmud *Bavli* did not want to present our El'azar (ben Hurcanus) to be noticed by peeping Christians looking for what they would maintain are blasphemous slurs. With the appropriate vowel markings ((subsumed into phonetic equivalents)) -------- <and absent such

markings the revised articulation was known to be the one which comes forth as "Eliezer"> ---- ---- there would be, in effect, a dodge whereby "Eliezer" would not automatically be associated with the "El'azar" who was tight with Yeshu.

In any case, the reality is that <u>there were NO disciples of Yeshu who held the name "Yochanan</u>."

> *. {The Fourth Gospel in its final redaction is -- at once -- ***the most Semitic of all the Gospel accounts; AND AT ONCE the most Anti-Semitic of all the Gospels.***
> The conundrum is easily adjudicated.
> El'azar ((he was still far away from being a Rabbi at this stage)) put "pen-to-ink" during his time at the Jerusalem Community.
> He kept his manuscript when he left the Jerusalem Community. Having been more or less cut out of his family ((the father had suspended his Patrimony)) he became a beggar in Jerusalem. One knows that El'azar ended up -- with the joint help of Rabbi Yochanan ben Tsakkai and of El'azar's father -- being a star in the *Beit ha Midrash* in Jerusalem headed by Tsakkai.
> Correlatively, his patrimony was re-instated.
> Writing the manuscript had helped him relieve himself from the influence of Yeshu.
> He automatically wrote as a Jew and all the tropisms of the manuscript were Jewish tropisms. He put it aside when he finished. He had considered burning it; but he decided to keep it. He, El'azar, wanted to have, for the record, the true figure of Yeshu to be accurate: *the good; the bad; and the ugly.*

When Rabbi El'azar (-----"Rabbi Eliezer" of the Talmud *Bavli* rendition of his name -----) was near death he confided this manuscript to his son "Rabbi Yehoshua" (named by El'azar in honor of one of the great pillars at Yavne).

This son of Rabbi El'azar, Rabbi Yehoshua <son of Rabbi El'azar/Eliezer>, eventually sold this manuscript. By now the Yeshu factor in Judaism was flat; no interest. El'azar's son didn't get much money for it. Somehow the manuscript eventually came into the hands of Ignatius of Antioch, a relatively early "Father of the Church." It took some time for the text <largely in Hebrew with after-the-fact insertions and addenda in Aramaic> to be translated into Greek.

This Ignatius of Antioch (as well as subsequent Fathers of the Church) took upon themselves to *"de-Judaize"* portions of the Jewish-oriented text which would be anathema for the direction taken by early Christianity. Further there were writers among the anti-Semitic "fathers of the church" who inserted anti-Semitic slurs visited upon "The Jews." All in all, this Fourth Gospel is, at once, the most Semitic of all the Gospels <insofar as the *ur*-document crafted by El'azar was fully Semitic and proudly Jewish>, and at once, the most Anti-Semitic of all the Gospels by virtue of incursions into the document over the next century and a-half, especially in Alexandria by way of the "Fathers" of the Church."

The manuscript was, in fact, the most reliable record of Yeshu's three-year ministry. ((In other words the manuscript celebrated what was the good, the bad, and the ugly about the Preacher. In this manuscript El'azar put himself forth as "the other disciple." {{{And in any case there was no "Yochanan" who was a follower of Yeshu; the "beloved disciple" was, simply, El'azar.}}}}

****

****

****

I feel like vomiting when I read about Saul/Paul. His Jewish credentials were thin. Some have suggested that Saul/Paul was a baby out of wedlock, the product of the father's shenanigans. This out-of-wedlock production was an embarrassment for the father. He looked ahead to the day when he would be free of this embarrassment; this *mamzer.* Saul/Paul's father gave to his out-of-wedlock son, as he became a young adult, a very generous stipend which would allow the *mamzer* to live well -------------- ***with the understanding that he would not return to the homestead***.

Saul/Paul was a nominal Jew. Unlike the other siblings of the family Saul/Paul -- *the mamzer** -- was not given a Jewish education. This *mamzer* dreamed of becoming famous. For a while he turned against his Jewish roots. Later he came in to contact with people who had met some disciples of Yeshu (who by this time was dead and buried for some time in Nazareth). He was puzzled by this 'Yeshu thing'. They promoted themselves as being special. Special was something which Saul/Paul lusted for but never had. He resented these "Yeshu-ites."

*. {The *mamzeratic* status of Saul/Paul and Yeshu were not the same. Yeshu was

born of a Jewish mother. Saul/Paul was the *mamzeratic* outcome of a father who was Jewish but a mother who was not Jewish.}

This Saul/Paul took it upon himself to suppress this 'Yeshu-thing." He killed some of them. One of his victims who was mortally injured by Saul/Paul offered, (offered as he was dying), the information that Yeshu was a *mamzer.*

This revelation changed everything. Finding out that a figure such as Yeshu who commanded SUCH respect even after he had died WAS A MAMZER! changed everything for Saul/Paul. **INSTANT TRANSFORMATION!!!!!**.

He made a full about-turn and started to praise this "leader" whom he had never encountered in the flesh. Indeed Saul/Paul virtually identified with this man from Nazareth even though he had never encountered Yeshu in the flesh. In other words, Saul/Paul ***created* a facsimile of Yeshu**, never having encountered him in person at all. More than that he turned against the enemies of those who followed the spirit of this "YESHU" figure.

*****

Something rotten was inculcated into early Christianity by virtue of these "epistles" of Saul/Paul. And, sadly, by and large the early Church ---- foolishly ---- sanctified these "epistles." The reality, however, is that these "epistles" were rife with Anti-Semitism. The template of these epistles <<<marinated viciously over the centuries>>> caused many Jews to be slaughtered *IN THE NAME OF GOD AND YESHU over the centuries.* Enough said.

*****

The reality was that Yeshu, had he been alive, would have been embarrassed <and enraged!> to have adulation from this kind of person. Yeshu had

his failings; some very, very significant. But Yeshu was not a killer; Yeshu was not a murderer.
The reality is that the Pauline influence came to be instantiated as, basically, an Anti-Semitic force. His growing influence ((inclusive of his "Letters" <and speaking as if he had years of acquaintance with Yeshu when in fact he had NEVER met Yeshu>)) mesmerized many. He certainly did not mesmerize Jews who quickly took his measure as an Anti-Semite. The emerging Christo-centric groupings -- and later with the Fathers of the Church -- were groupings which were largely Anti-Semitic. Christianity was born in the cesspool of Anti-Semitism.
Frankly, the deepest seeds of Anti-Semitism -- orchestrated by many but none more than Saul/Paul -- are found in the "Letters" of Saul/Paul. The whole dynamic here, over the centuries, turned out to be a dynamic which allowed for *AUSHWITCH*.]
****
****
****
****
****

Mark
14: 50 -- 52.

And they all left him and fled. Now a young man followed him wearing nothing but a linen cloth about his body. They seized him, but he left the cloth behind and ran off naked.

What's going on here? Listen:
Caiaphas was in a HUGE quandary. The "Plan" was in smithereens. Yeshu had utterly been changed ever since the fraud 'resurrection.' But something much deeper than that was at issue. Yeshu realized that the whole *hokus-pokus* of that crazy scheme had the horrific -- and unintended -- outcome that

Miriam went to pieces when her beloved brother "died" and was buried. For the four days before Yeshu arrived at the homestead Miriam said nothing and ate nothing; she sipped water. She seemed to be a zombie hearing nothing and seeing nothing with her eyes open. When Yeshu finally arrived and met with the zombie-esque Miriam he knew that even the forth-coming "miraculous resurrection" would change nothing for Miriam: **she had EXPERIENCED the death of her beloved younger brother.** Yeshu also realized that the fraud "resurrection" would actually push Miriam <<that is, if she were able to function at all>> to a greater and dangerous depression. ((And indeed, Miriam never returned to her normal way.)) She was a Zombie. Period. And she died an early death. As we have seen above this set of developments awakened Yeshu to the mostly narcissistic character of his "ministry." He felt ashamed and cried like a baby when it fully dawned on him that his "ministry" was not at all a true "ministry." In many ways, he now understood, that his very **self** was fraudulent. Indeed the forthcoming sham "resurrection" would be nothing more than the very epitome of fraudulence.

All of this constituted for Yeshu what might be referred to as a *metanoia*. He resolved to himself that he would do what he could do such that no-one of his closest associates and no-one of the ones he loved (El'azar especially) would not have to pay the price for **his** machinations. He was, now, a truly changed man. A man determined to be killed in such a fashion that his close associates would not have to take on the burden.* Yeshu, after knowing what had happened to Miriam, wanted no-one at all to suffer because of his narcissistic "ministry." And to his credit he pulled it off. He was the only one who really suffered for that ridiculous fraud "resurrection." He did not always live nobly; not by a long-shot. But most certainly he died nobly.

*. {{Of course Caiaphas -- who midwifed "The Plan" – also bears a certain amount of responsibility for this outcome. First of all, it was foolish to begin with to make the unstable Yeshu the center-piece (along with that young boy) of "The Plan." On the other hand, one must understand that Caiphas had set in motion "The Plan" as a way of siphoning-off the revolutionary fervor among the young men of Jerusalem (((so many of them were in Jerusalem because of the onerous conditions of the horrific Roman Occupation))). Caiaphas understood that if these young Jews were to actually challenge the Roman might Jerusalem would be decimated. Siphoning-off of the revolutionary fervor of these young men without a future ***could*** -- just possibly -- might coalesce around the figure of Yeshu. After all Yeshu had an uncanny way of inspiring a following. The long shot was this: In the first place he, Yeshu, was one of them <i.e., the poor and disenfranchised> by his background. But the Preacher also had the ability to bring enthusiasm to these poor and disenfranchised centered on a charismatic figure. Just possibly revolutionary fervor could be exchanged for religious fervor. After all Caiaphas would arrange something stupendously fervent which would give meaning to these poor and disenfranchised Jews <a fair amount with families>.

Thus "The Plan."

The charismatic figure named Yeshu was critical to "The Plan." Again, he was one of them. And lo-and-behold! Caiaphas would orchestrate something which would put these poor and disenfranchised Jews on a pedestal. To wit:

Yeshu "—one of "them" -- would function as a High Priest for the poor and disenfranchised. This figure would hold the nomenclature of "The High Priest" for the poor and disenfranchised. This figure would be ordained such that this "High Priest for the Poor and Disenfranchised" would be allowed to enter in the HOLY OF HOLIES ON *YOM KIPPUR* AND **ARTICULATE ALOUD THE SACRED NAME** <from the true name as per *Exodus* 3:14>; {{{with the understanding that the four-lettered name in 3:15 was a clever dodge; a clever circumlocution which non-Jews could fixate upon thinking that they were articulating the NAME}}}.

Of course, on the same day, but at a different time, it would be the High Priest who would orchestrate the same ceremony on *Yom Kippur.*}}**

*****

> **. {{The best laid plans often go amiss. There were unforeseen variables which would, in effect, blow "The Plan" to smithereens.
>
> First and foremost, no one took into account of Miriam who **DOTED** on El'azar. She ***EXPERIENCED***, in her mind, the death of her beloved brother. She never recovered; not even when it became evident that: i). Putatively he was resurrected; and

worse, to find out that the whole thing was a scam; a "one/two" punch from which she never recovered.}}

***** ***** ***** ***** *****

Returning back to El'azar for a moment.
El'azar was well aware that something huge was going to happen that Thursday night (followed, of course by the events of Friday). HUGE! Yes. But exactly what was to transpire was not certain <at least to El'azar and the regular disciples. There was much confusion in the air. As much as he could, El'azar wanted to stay in the near vicinity of Yeshu -------- but in such a way that he could "escape" if matters became too dangerous. The arrest of Yeshu brought shivers to his spine.

***** ***** *****

Caiaphas.
The "Plan" had been blown to smithereens. The fraud Resurrection did not, in the final analysis, achieve what was hoped for; indeed, just the opposite.

Caiaphas could not fathom at all what Yeshu was up to. He was not in character at all. Now that Yeshu's actions had blown 'The Plan' to smithereens Caiaphas was not sure what to do. And time was running out. The "Great Shabbat" was near; very near. The matter would have to be settled one way or another in less than thirty-six hours.
The more Caiaphas dwelled on what was going on with Yeshu he, Caiaphas, started to understand that Yeshu -- full of remorse for what happened to Miriam -- wanted to die. There could be no other explanation for this radical change which came over Yeshu.

But there was also another factor than the slow demise of Miriam.

"The Plan" had, back then, gone to Yeshu's endemic narcissism. He had done many amazing things during his ministry. But the participating in THE PLAN went to his head. He became even more "electric" knowing what was in store for him when *Yom Kippur* would come again. He became reckless, especially with his carelessness relative to the NAME.

Now it became more clear to Caiaphas that there was a deep erratic streak in Yeshu; indeed a very dangerous streak as Yeshu looked forward to "The Great Shabbat."

Yeshu's blasphemies (((i.e., claiming THE FATHER AND I ARE ONE; and his clever usage of the four-letter NAME of God from Exodus 3:14 and which he sometimes deployed as a trivial "I-am" thinking that such was clever))) was truly a HUGE stain on the figure of Yeshu. On the one hand the four-letter Name of God was sacred. But technically the same four lettered word could also -- technically -- be as a natural statement <although this usage of the four lettered word without the context of the NAME of God was hardly ever deployed in fact>. Thus Yeshu could present himself as "I-am" in a trivial sense almost as tease. At the same time the phrasing carried the import of triviality OR the input of the most Sacred NAME of God. It was foolish of him to treat "the Name" in this fashion. Caiaphas had heard of such shenanigans and it did not please Caiaphas at all. How dare he downgrade the Sacred Name!

Caiaphas settled on the following. He would bring Yeshu to the "meeting room" (functioning as a

rump-Sanhedrin in a manner of saying) and put him on the spot.
As Caiaphas ruminated on all these things he called to mind a Jewish Proverb:

It is better for one man to die for the People than for the whole nation be destroyed.

Fast forward to the "rump Sanhedrin."

*****

Turning back to Mark's Gospel.

Mark

14: 50 -- 52.

And they all left him and fled. Now a young man followed him wearing nothing but a linen cloth about his body. They seized him, but he left the cloth behind and ran off naked.

Let us now put in perspective this piece of information from *Mark* 14: 50--52.
The four gospel accounts are not symmetrical; indeed the four accounts of the arrest, the trial, and the outcome **are wildly a-symmetrical**.
If we stay with the Markan account we might surmise that this "young man" was, indeed, El'azar. There were some restive tangles involving the arrest of Yeshu. Grabbing someone's covering (leaving only a linen cloth covering his privates <which ALSO came to be stripped from him>) -- say, El'azar's -- could easily be the case. Doubtlessly this young aristocrat had a servant with him who managed to supply sufficient clothing to the naked El'azar.

*****

In any case, we have seen, that El'azar was let into the "rump"-*Sanhedrin* by virtue of his hailing from that wealthy and honored family living in Bethany. His family was well known. We have also noted that Shimon 'The Rock' was with him. Without El'azar there would be no chance in hell for this head of the "rag-tag" grouping of the disciples of Yeshu being in the 'meeting room' wherein this rump *Sanhendrin* took place. We have also noted that -- anyway -- Shimon 'The Rock' was subsequently escorted out before the actual trial led by Caiaphas, the High Priest. El'azar, however, stayed the whole time.

*****

The Great Shabbat was approaching. One way or another he, Caiaphas, had to resolve this scandalous situation. He put in motion a plan by which Yeshu could redeem himself or could ruin himself. He would have Yeshu arrested and have Yeshu explain his actions for himself. Caiaphas had made this plan on what might be called an unofficial Sanhedrin trial. To be sure, the rump-Sanhedrin under the Roman Occupation had no authority at all for putting any Jew to death. (((And a fortiori the charge of Blasphemy with respect to the Jewish God would most surely laughed out of any Roman hearing or court.))

Caiaphas understood such and he was well aware that nothing would happen without the "OK" of Pilate. But we are getting ahead of our story.

Yeshu was in a death spiral of his own making. He still carried the pain for what had transpired by virtue of that sham "Resurrection." Miriam, it was clear, would never really return to the living. Yeshu wanted to die, one way or another.

His comportment at the rump *Sandrehin* made matters worse. Caiaphas did not know what to do. He decided to force the issue. Caiaphas certainly knew about the blasphemy of several weeks ago when the leaders of the Pharasaic Sect, here, and, there, Yeshu swapped insults to each other. And, indeed, the report was that Yeshu had brazenly retorted* the jibes visited upon by virtue of his *mamzer* status. Allegedly the rumor had spread

that Yeshu had brazenly articulated allowed the four-lettered name of God from *Exodus* 3:14.
But this was second hand material. Caiaphas wanted to have a face-to-face so that, one way or another, the matter would be adjudicated. It would be up to Yeshu himself to save himself or to, in effect, execute himself.
Yeshu (predictably) did not cooperate with --- or even answer with any substance -- to all of his accusers other than Caiaphas.
Caiaphas knew that Yeshu was clever; he, Caiaphas, would have to go straight to the heart of the matter. He would give Yeshu an out. Yes his public blasphemy was well known. But tonight Caiaphas would put the key question to him: **Who do you say you are?** If Yeshu were to reiterate the blasphemy he would set in motion the death of Yeshu by means of the Roman Procurator.
All the Jews in the meeting-room (functioning as a rump *Sanhedrin*) would know that the charge was blasphemy. But Caiaphas would present before Pilate a crime dealing with the Jewish expectation of the *Moshiah*. In the revolutionary background in Jerusalem a *Moshiah* would most certainly be a powerful leader which would free *Erets Yisrael* from the hated Roman Occupation. If Yeshu allowed himself to be a Messianic figure face-to-face to Pilate, he would surely be put to death.
On the other hand, if Yeshu eschewed his prior blasphemies, he would go free.
*****
Getting back to the meeting-room of the rump *Sanhedrin*. What would Yeshu say in response to Caiaphas' direct query?: **Who do you say you are?** The answer was clear and fully blasphemous: what Yeshu articulated **aloud** was the sacred four-lettered NAME **OF GOD!!!!** from *Exodus* 3:**14**.
*****

So Yeshu was remanded to the graces of Pilate. The interrogation by Pilate was totally with respect to whether or not Yeshu had Messianic claims. Yeshu answered the messianic charges ambiguously, and, to other questions Yeshu put forth to Pilate answers which puzzled Pilate. Pilate could not extract from the Galilean a straight answer. Pilate was flustered. Pilate only had one other option: a Roman Whipping. The "whip" was equipped with sharp iron pieces embedded in the wide lash. It was truly diabolical. Would it be so punishing such that Yeshu would be putty in the hands of Pilate? That's what Pilate was hoping for. Not a chance in hell. Yeshu had crossed the line; he wanted to die.

When Yeshu returned to Pilate he had blood all over his body. Pilate re-interrogated the prisoner. Yeshu answers were fuzzy and in any case his fuzzy answers did not at all fit the template of a military Messiah.

Pilate, then, literally, washed his hands of the Yeshu matter. He remanded the bloodied and deeply scarred body -- still alive -- to be brought back to Caiaphas with the caveat that his rump *Sanhedrin* could take whatever measures It wanted. In effect -- but not "officially" -- Pilate was giving Caiaphas a free hand. He knew that Caiaphas would bring a capital charge (in Jewish Law) against Yeshu. The onus would be on Caiaphas, not on him.

Caiaphas, when he saw Yeshu, had to excuse himself. He vomited. He knew this was ugly stuff. But Blasphemy --- especially the way Yeshu pursued it on this night -- **<u>was also ugly stuff</u>**.

Hanging from a Tree was -- in Jewish Law -- the penalty for Blasphemy. But the Roman Government would not cooperate with such an

outcome since this BLASPHEMY had no standing in Roman Law. The default would be that -- based on the ambiguities involved in the interchanges between Pilate and Yeshu -- this Yeshu from Nazareth had Messianic aspirations. That would qualify for a death penalty under Roman Law. The default for capital punishment was Crucifixion. And a ROMAN Crucifixion was the most diabolical punishment which one could imagine. And that's what happened to Yeshu.
****
****
****
****
****

repetitio mater studiorum
resiliation is the father of truth

Rabbi El'azar (some say "Eliezer") hailed from a rich family in Bethany. He was the one who would be referred (in the Fourth Gospel) to as "the other disciple." El'azar had been a close associate with Yeshu when he, El'azar, was a young adolescent. He was never one of the putative "twelve," by his own choice. He was something of an on-again/ off-again "disciple." But even Shimon, "The Rock," deferred to him.
*****
"The other disciple." He was Yeshu's favorite even though he was not a regular. And Yeshu spent a lot of time in Bethany and had a close relationship with one of El'azar's two sisters: the one called Miriam (which was the namesake of Yeshu's mother). The other was the sister of Miriam -- Martha -- who, to her credit, was always, from the beginning, skeptical of the charming Preacher. For

Martha, something was definitely 'off' about this man but she could never put it into words. She felt sorry that her brother had become so consumed with this guy.
El'azar, as it will have been, ended up as the center-piece of a scandalous bit of outrageous nonsense in Bethany.

What was at stake {"The Plan"} was a "top secret" orchestration which would transform this very popular guy from Nazareth into a "High Priest for the Poor and Disenfranchised." In that capacity, he would be graced with the honor of entering into the Holy of Holies in the Temple on *Yom Kippur* and articulate aloud THE NAME. The High Priest, Caiaphas, had hatched the plan and cleared it with Pilate. It would, according to 'the plan,' siphon off the Revolutionary fervor of the poor and disenfranchised who, bereft of money and work, just crowded into the Capital.
When the time came for the fraud* "Resurrection" {{{i.e., the planned sudden upsurge of the status of Yeshu; after all, his other putative "near resurrections" were not really convincing}}}

Yeshu followed through with the scam in the sense of going through the motions. His heart was no longer in "The Plan." See below. After all his beloved El'azar would now be saddled as being a fraud. But Yeshu orchestrated things such that he alone would own the guilt. The hope was that if **he** – i.e., Yeshu-- followed through as owning the fraudulent "resurrection" there would be less interest in El'azar. (((On the other hand, when this "glorious" Resurrection would eventually be unmasked as a fraud El'azar would still be saddled with being a fraud, anyway.)))
****
****

There had been much planning for this fraud Resurrection which -- if it were "successful" -- would usher in the goal of "The Plan."

The reality was that Yeshu's prior journey to Eygpt had made Yeshu something of an expert in the "magical" arts and, as well, he purchased potions and the like whereby "a magician" could induce what would appear to be the stopping of breathing and, correlatively, such a magician using another potion, could resuscitate the one who -- so it would appear -- had stopped breathing. In the beginning of his "ministry" these feats seemed to be miraculous. But over time the routine became transparent. Yeshu had lost some of his admirers. But the Caiaphas-spawned "Plan" was one which would change -- that was the hope -- the deteriorating situation in the Capital. Caiaphas understood that something had to be done -- and quickly -- to avoid some revolt in the capital. Potions and mesmerizing would not be sufficient. But something **HUGE** had to be deployed to calm the revolutionary fever which permeated Jerusalem. And let's be clear: anything smacking of a military challenge to the Roman Occupation would have set in motion a blood-fest wherein the living would envy the dead. <<And of course, about thirty-thirty-five years later such a bloodbath became real AND, "as a bonus," the Temple was decimated.>>

Continuing on:

Only something **HUGE** (if successful) would catalyze the disenfranchised to sense that they -- the disenfranchised Jews simmering with dreams of Revolt -- could be actual players. But the catalytic event would have to be both HUGE – and – have the aura of credulity about it.

How about if Yeshu were miles away when El'azar was buried? How about El'azar being in the tomb for FOUR DAYS? Would all that be convincing enough? Keep in mind that the tomb for El'azar was large, spacious, and above ground. It was the kind of tomb which only rich people could afford. It was the kind of cave-tomb wherein trusted servants (with a death-threat if they screwed up and/or mentioned this to others) could bring to the "deceased" El'azar food, drink, and the wherewithal for sanitary conditions within the tomb.

*****

This was to be the closer. Yeshu was miles away during those four days. That was part of the plan.

We will cite the passage from *John* 11:11 – 16. Yeshu was tipping his hand. **FOUR DAYS IN THE TOMB!!!** There would be no way to compare his earlier resuscitations with this stupendous "resurrection" **AFTER FOUR DAYS DEAD IN THE TOMB**. Listen:

Our beloved El'azar is resting. I am going to wake him.

The disciples said to him:

Adonai! If he is able to rest he is sure to get better.

[The phrase Yeshu used with reference to the death of El'azar was ambiguous since they thought that by 'rest' he <Yeshu> meant 'sleep.' So Yeshu put it plainly:

El'azar is dead

AND FOR YOUR SAKE I AM GLAD (!) ***THAT I WAS NOT THERE BECAUSE NOW YOU WILL*** [finally] ***BELIEVE****

*. I have the impression that Yeshu was peevish insofar as his followers didn't get the point right away. And, indeed, there was surely some skepticism about a resurrection after four days in the tomb. But if you think it through it turned out that he, Yeshu, was, in fact, not to be believed.

****
****

So. Yeshu actually did follow through with the sham "resurrection" but now with a dramatically changed agendum. There was one factor which had escaped both Yeshu and Caiaphas in their planning. An unforeseen factor which, in the final analysis, would (right away for some; with time, virtually all) render this to be the lowest and lewdliness farce of the century; perhaps the lowest farce of all time.
Prior to the farce 'resurrection' Miriam had a breakdown. Younger than Martha but older than El'azar, Miriam had been irretrievably devastated by the "death" of her beloved younger brother. Miriam was irretrievably devastated by the "death" <<for her IT WAS REAL AND IT BROKE HER SPIRIT FOR GOOD>>.

When Yeshu arrived four days posterior to the "death" of El'azar Yeshu understood immediately that the "resurrection" of El'azar would be even more devastating to Miriam insofar as the whole thing would, rather quickly, morph into the service of **a "'freaking," stupid disaster, all around**. How tawdry! And how devastating! She had been psychically blown away irretrievably by his "death."

AND THEN to find out that the whole thing was a hoax! She would never again be what she had been. In many ways, her life was over.

Yeshu had cried like a baby after his meeting with Miriam. This was *his* awakening.

To Yeshu's credit he looked deeply into his soul for the first time. His whole "ministry" was -- at base -- one of self-aggrandizement. When he returned to Bethany (i.e., after the four days of the "burial' of El'azar) he was stunned by his self-revelation of how tawdry he had become in general and how willingly he had agreed to a "plan" which could only work by making himself the center of a ghastly fraud. By the time he arrived after four days of burial for El'azar it was the run-up to the climatic "Great Shabbat" <i.e., falling on the first day of *Pesach*>. Yeshu, now, was deep into a death-wish even as the crowds on the road to Jerusalem were in a frenzy to celebrate what they perceived to be the ***Mosiah*** who had finally arrive. {{{They would, of course, find out the tawdry reality.}}}
Yeshu followed through with his now radically *stupid* "plan" to bring about his wish. To his credit Yeshu understood that if he, Yeshu, were to have totally (and deeply embarrassingly to all involved) scotched "the Plan" it would be El'azar -- whom he loved the most -- would suffer the most.
Of course he, Yeshu, would have to face the music as well. Yeshu eschewed any grandeur ((one of the planned outcomes according to the original scenario)). All of this was radically contrary to the plan. First with the shocked Caiaphas and then with the deeply puzzled Pilate. As it would turn out -- to the surprise of all including Caiaphas and Pilate -- Yeshu managed to fulfill his final wish <<i.e., to have himself alone <excepting, of course, Miriam

who would never be the same again> pay the consequence of that stupid fraud>>.
****
****
****

{{Codicil to the Above}}
El'azar was there in Caiaphas' meeting-room. He had no trouble getting in when the doorman recognized who he was. That night El'azar was with Shimon 'the Rock' who more or less was the Head of the grouping of Yeshu's followers. Because he was with El'azar Shimon 'the Rock' was let in as well. As it would turn out, El'azar was there for the whole time before Yeshu was shunted over to Pilate and through the inquisition. Not so lucky for Shimon 'the Rock.' It became clear that he was one of the "rag-tie' followers of Yeshu. He was escorted out of the meeting room.
This meeting-room was functioning more or less as a rump *Sanhedrin*. The matter at hand was a capital punishment <<<Blasphemy, in Jewish Law, was a capital offence>>>. There was no possibility at all that the Roman Occupation would allow for this "trial" outcome ----- even if Yeshu was convicted of a capital crime in Jewish Law. Blasphemy in this case ---- according to Jewish Law -- was a capital wrong punishable by death by hanging from a tree. However, by virtue of the Roman Occupation, this *rump*-Sanhedrin had no power at all to execute the one who was found guilty. Any Jew (in this case Yeshu) who committed a capital crime was beyond the authority of the Jewish officials. Caiaphas understood this. If this rump Sanhedrinesque trial found Yeshu to have committed Blasphemy <<indeed, several times in public>> there would have to be another way of bringing a capital crime against Yeshu. These Jewish matters

were taken very seriously by the Jews. But these Jewish matters were not **at all** recognized under Roman Law.

As we shall see below, clever Caiaphas had Yeshu shunted over to Pilate ***with however*** a crime which may or may not have been committed by Yeshu: that Yeshu was presenting himself as the *Moshiach*. For the Roman officials such a claim would FOR SURE put him to death, by the Roman Procurator since it was well disseminated in Jewish belief that the Messianic promise would take the form of a military figure. If Yeshu were to claim messianic status, he most certainly would have been put to death by Pilate <<<<And, recall here, the rump *Sanhedrin* didn't even bring up the possibility of Yeshu being the Messiah. Caiaphas understood that Pilate didn't care a rat's ass about Jewish concerns relative to Blasphemy. Caiaphas was hoping that Pilate himself would bring up the one thing about this Jew which would be germane>>>>

So Pilate washed his hands of the whole (and crazy) *imbroglio*. He simply sent Yeshu back to Caiaphas saying, in effect, to Caiaphas: ***This whole nonsense is YOUR JEWISH MATTER. Do with him as you will. But under NO circumstances are you*** (Caiaphas and that rump-*Sanhedrin*) ***to bring this matter to me again.***

*****

For the record:

What transpired in the "meeting room" was, unofficially of course, something like a rump-*Sanhedrin* <insofar as a "true" meeting of the *Sanhedrin* dealing with capital punishment could not be allowed by the Roman Occupation> on that night which would be before the night which would inaugurate both the Shabbat and *Pesach*.

****

****

****

****

****

****

Shame on the Synoptics

Say it is November 22/23 in Dallas, Texas.
Try to imagine that there were no newspaper reports, radio broadcasts, or television presentations of the Kennedy Assassination.
How could that happen? What kind of suppression would allow for THAT!
I bring up this false possibility to make a point.
By far and away the most dramatic event for Yeshu, his followers; his enemies; and the curious; **was that stupid orchestrated "resurrection" at Bethany.**
So: Just what was the coverage in Matthew's Gospel of this most dramatic event for Yeshu; for El'azar; for Caiaphas; and hordes of Jews spewing Palms on the road from Bethany to Jerusalem while Yeshu rode on a donkey <albeit in a somber mood in the midst of all this excitement>? NONE AT ALL!
NOT A PEEP!
And, of course, the sophisticated LUKE Gospel wouldn't even come close to allowing even a hint that there was anything like fully orchestration of a fraud "resurrection." And likewise for the account in Mark, albeit without the sophistication
The whole thing was suppressed in the final versions of each of the Synoptics; **TOTALLY SKIPPING OVER THE MOST DRAMATIC AND MOST CONSEQUENTIAL DEVELOPMENT IN THE THREE YEAR MINISTRY OF YESHU'S LIFE.**

The silence of the Synoptics is thunderous. Let it sink in. Learn from this. Sometimes what is NOT said is orders of magnitude of significance than what was said.
****
****
****
****

OBSERVATIONS:
"Of course I understand. I am not as *"dufus"* as you take me to be. OF COURSE I understand that the Gospel of a (putative) 'John' is the latest of the Four Gospels. OF COURSE I understand that this most authentic of the Gospels was "graced" <<more like "subjected to">> with an Hellenic quasi-philosophic overlay: <<*In the Beginning*; "LOGOS" for God's sake!!!! AND HOW TAWDRY!!!>>. You can't get more Hellenic than that.
This overlay is totally at odds with the **deeply Semitic*** character of this Gospel. There are several things which must be addressed with regard to the deeply Semitic character of the *ur*text <<produced by El'azar in his time in the Jerusalem Community headed by Jacob, the half-brother of Yeshu>> of this fourth Gospel which then, paradoxically and pathologically, is melded by the early Fathers of the Church into in the same text which renders the Fourth Gospel, as the most Anti-Semitic Gospel. Without a doubt, had El'azar <who had been dead for a number of decades before these matters surfaced> the one who penned the original accounting of Yeshu while at the *min* called "The Jerusalem Community" would have burned his own production (which was no-longer his by a long shot) insofar as the poison interjected into the that original manuscript vilifies this Fourth Gospel.

*****

But by this time (Rabbi El'azar was dead about five years before what would eventually be called the end of the first century <ce>) the *ur*-production was being subjected to the *emerging Ethos* of the early Fathers of the Church. It was the "Fathers of the Church" (((who were desperately attempting to "launch" a set of "doctrines" <<<"doctrines" which were -- to take a phrase from another time -- *Juden-Frie* -- and which were indeed foreign to Judaism>>> which would be the "structure" of this new religion which they were creating.

And, in one sense, that's fair, after all. They were creating out of "thin-air" "doctrines" bereft of Judaism. And that's OK if you were only playing a fiddle. Any Jewish readers would quickly push such nonsense aside.

What was NOT OK -- indeed it stains every dimension of this new created religion -- was their massive interjection of Anti-Semitism into this "Fourth Gospel." The lasting roots of this vile and ingrained pathology emerged, as we have seen earlier, were those vicious "Letters" of Saul/Paul the creator of "Anti-Semitism."

> *. {Don't get that confused with "Anti-Semitic." OF COURSE I understand that the fourth Gospel is rife with an overlay of Anti-Semitism <generated by those "Fathers of the Church" well after the original composition (i.e., El'azar's *ur*-document) of this **most Semitic** of all the Gospels>.
> In turn there was the Hellenic overlay occurring roughly a century posterior to the demise of Yeshu. This Hellenic overlay emerged in Alexandria right at the time when the Anti-Semitic "Fathers of the Church" started to create a Church which was to be distinguished, as much as is

possible, from the true Jewish origins of Yeshu. The somewhat "gushy" portrayals of Yeshu in all four Gospels belies both the strengths and weaknesses of Yeshu.
Say whatever you want to say -- encomia or castigations -- about Yeshu, the fact will remain forever that this troubled man was born as a Jew; lived as a Jew; and died as a Jew. Period. He was certainly not founding a new Church or new Religion.}

****
****
****

PART TWO.

An Observation:

I am projecting to my hoped audience of Jews --- and Orthodox Jews in particular--- a very different accounting of Judaism in general; an accounting with emphasis on Scripture, first and foremost. And then there are the more nuanced offerings of portions of our Talmud *Bavli* produced by those subtle "final anonymous editors" of our *Bavli* from roughly 575 to roughly 610ce. Subtlety was the only coinage in this orchestration by the 'final anonymous editors'. The over-arching power of Rabbinic Officialdom could be checked only by subtle and indirect insertions into "The Record" by our glorious *final editors of the* Talmud *Bavli*. God bless them.

Take heed:

I am quite consciously attempting to strip you of multiple presuppositions which -- if those presuppositions permeate your reading of this production -- would give you a false understanding of what I am putting forth.

I fully realize that my presentation of these things is not the "received" presentation of these things. So when you first read it you are likely to presume that I am <<-- like a dufus without any consciousness of such -->> akin to of, say, a "bar Hei Hei" <or one of those "heretics" which populate so much of *Genesis Rabbah*>> thereby giving one a good conscience to quickly dismiss my accounting of things Jewish. **It is absolutely amazing how people entrenched in a received tradition _do not really HEAR_ what is being offered to them when it comes from a perspective to which they are not habituated. There is only one way to break that ugly danger:**

repetitio mater studiorum

resiliationin the father of truth

Take it or leave it. The burden is now on you.

****

****

****

****

****

****

When pre-existing Theology interferes with the natural meaning of Scripture, it only means that the Theology is defective.

To wit: Plotinus.

It is a trap. The Plotinian model conjures a majesty which turns out to be something of, literally, a *faux pas*: "a false step."

For many, and apparently for Yadin, Plotinus instantiates this false theology for many Jews, here; for most Christians, there; and for many Muslims, there. For these Plotinian-esque types (and Yadin is one of them) this frame of reference is the "received theology" <even for those who never heard of Plotinus>. To wit and staccatically:

WOW!!! Beyond Being! ***OH MY GOD!!!!!*** *A One which transcends the human ability to know it, and likewise, transcends the human ability to give it articulation!!!!* ***Wow!*** *An "a-peiron"* [aka: *AYN-SOF!* aka "In-Finitus"] *which -- even though it cannot be understood by the human mind nor articulated by human language -- is SOMEHOW* **KNOWN** *to "overflow" in ten levels of emanation which poetic Jewish thinkers* [starting in Provence towards the of the eleventh century] *will Hebraize* {{and, I must say, with greater pizazz than Plotinus himself}} *as Siferot*!!!!!
Thus was born a new wrinkle in Philosophy [and, for that matter, a new wrinkle for Jewish Studies]. Some claim that such goes back to Plato. Indeed this is how Plotinus understood it. However, any fair study of Plato will show that this Plotinian schema is not the true and final Platonic position. Yes, Plato, in *Republic* did articulate a "GOOD" which was *epikeina tes ousias* {"beyond being"}. But the final accounting of Plato's "GOOD" had nothing in common with the Plotinian schema <and, for that matter nothing in common with the original "*epikeina tes ousias*"> articulated by Plato. All things considered what is usually often referred to as "Neo-Platonic" should really be referred to as "Neo-Plotinian."
*****
Thus was born a NEW orientation in these matters albeit many claim that it comes from Plato.* There is some truth in that; but Plato's final accounting of "The Good" has nothing in common with the *AYN-SOF* of Plotinus.

> *. {Yes. Plato's original accounting of "the Good" was married to what, much later, would be gathered together under the *via negativa* orientation: "***epikeina tes ousias***" <albeit not using that term {i.e., "via

> negativa"} which term <*via negativa*> came much later in the history of Philosophy>. But as Plato matured into his later period of Philosophy he jettisoned his own wording <*epikeina tes ousias*> as found in *Republic Sixth* in favor of a **generative** meaning of "the good." This evolution of "the good" in Plato's late productions ((along with helping -- after the fact -- inserts into the original version of "the good" in *Republic Six*)). Yes. A **generative** offspring (i.e.: **TOKOS**: Child or Offspring)). You must attend to my "Jerusalem and Athens" production to understand this clearly.

*****

Accordingly, there was born a TURN in Philosophy which is the invention of Plotinus but which is -- inaccurately in the final analysis -- foolishly credited to Plato. ((In other words: Plato initially, in *Republic VI*, did, in effect deploy language which pointed to the *via negativa* orientation <albeit that phrase was not Plato's; and, as we shall see, Plato withdrew from that orientation>. Thus was born a huge change in the History of Philosophy. However, towards the end of his life Plato jettisoned this frame of reference. In other words Plato came to eschew that orientation; Plato in his later years, that means, eschewed his "*epikeina tes ousias*" articulation.

Nonetheless what Plato himself jettisoned was, unfortunately, NOT jettisoned in the subsequent history of Philosophy. Indeed Plotinus traded on Plato's prior *epikeina tes ousias* as per *Republic-VI*. Accordingly, the "via negativa" became an embedded trope for the "Religions of Revelation" (i.e., Judaism; Christianity; and Islam). And, accordingly, this development was incorporated,

in various ways and at various times, into the understanding of Jews and their God; into the understanding of Christians and their God; and into Muslims and their God.
The truth is that each of these major religions were, in effect, denigrated to the extent that they married themselves to the *via negativa*.
*****
And here is the germane point:
One prong (of several prongs) of this whole nexus in Jewish Letters <i.e., the generic "*via negativa*" orientation> came to be known as "Qabbala."
However, it is true, that one can be a "via negativa" thinker without the baubles of Qabbala.
To be sure, one can put forth <and has put forth> a Jewish "via negativa" frame of reference for a Jewish Theology ***without*** the baubles of Qabbala.
Likewise ((and more sadly since ANY kind of "via negativa" orientation is not in tune with Scripture's accounting of God)) there can be and has been Jewishly-oriented "via negativa" orientations WITH the baubles of Qabbala.
I doubt that Yadin has given himself over to the version of the *via negativa* by way of the baubles of *Qabbala*. But he most certainly bonded himself to the generic orientation of the *via negativa* thereby missing the plain sense of the Scriptural accounting of God. To be sure, there are many apparitions of "God" in our *TaNaH*. But none of those models instantiate the *via negativa* orientation <<albeit Jews such as Yadin force their love affair with the *via negative* such that they mangle the plain sense of Scripture in order to "discover" in Scripture their treasured *via negativa*>>. Such is an exercise in "gross bad faith."

So? Everybody -- some would think -- has a right to this or that frame of reference even when it comes to Jewish Theology. But is that true? Listen to these wise words from the mouths of those who -- over the centuries maintained that the only **TRUE** Jewish Theology is a Theology firmly rooted in Scripture's *plain sense*. This has been alluded to in this undertaking and in many of my other undertakings. By this standard, the *via negativa* accounting of God is an accounting of a false God. **Let that sink in: A FALSE GOD**.

The Yadin faction and other versions of a Jewish *via negativa* God concept brings with it a network of concepts which, at root, vitiates the God of Scripture. And that is the problem. Very simply: the putative Yadinian notion of the Jewish God ***is in this*** **via negativa** ***mode***. An austere God. A sorry consequence of this "via-negativa" orientation. Interestingly enough, the best presentation of our true Jewish God, authored by *HASHEM*, is virtually the antipode of that stark resonations of the "via-negativa" orientation. It is found in Scripture. *Devarim* 30:11--14. To wit:

For this mitsva *I am laying down for you today is neither obscure for you nor beyond your reach. It is not in the heavens so that you need to wonder:* "Who will go up the heavens and bring it down for us." *Nor is it beyond the seas such that you would say:* "Who will cross the seas to get it for us and tell us of it."

NO:

It is something near to you: in your mouth and in your heart to put it in practice.

****

****

****

****

****

****
****
****

Yeshu, of course, was fathered by Pantera, the Sidonian archer who was drafted into the Roman army.

***** ***** ***** ***** *****

***** ***** *****

***** ***** ***** ***** *****

Fast forward:

By this time (i.e., the time of the beginning of the Gemara on the Mishna and sustained into the beginning of the seventh century) the Roman Church would scour as much as they could the manuscripts of these Gemaric productions. And it continued onto the Christian Middle Ages. Burning the manuscripts by Christian Zealots occurred often enough. Over time the writers of our *Bavli* became nuanced, especially with regard to names so that the Christian snoopers would not recognize important names. In this case "Pantera" became "Pandira."

****
****

The Empty Tomb.

There were two half-brothers of Yeshu among that "rag-tag" set of disciples who followed Yeshu: Yehuda and Shimon <<but not the Shimon who was known as "The Rock">>. They were shocked and somewhat disgusted with what Yeshu did at Bethany. They too knew how this whole fraudulent farce affected Miriam, the younger sister of El'azar. Yeshu himself would not respond to their overtures for ironing things out. And both of them -- Yehuda and Shimon -- had the sense that Yeshu was taking a turn towards self-destruction. The only person who could speak to Yeshu on an equal footing with Yeshu (at this point in his life) was his half-brother, Jacob, who was less than a year younger than Yeshu and who was very close to his slightly older half-brother. Prior to his decision to be a Preacher he would -- back in Nazareth -- come to Jacob when he, Yeshu, was in a depressed mood. <<This was a common problem with Yeshu.>> But now Jacob was in Nazareth and Yeshu was in Jerusalem.

Yehuda, the Treasurer of the rag-tag Group, used the money to hire out two horses so that they could get to Jacob and get Jacob to come down from Nazareth with them as soon as possible. When they reached Nazareth they were welcomed warmly. Jacob had missed them dearly. The two brothers, Yehuda and Shimon, told him about the hoax; about Miriam's irreversible Breakdown; and the uncanny -- perhaps even self-destructive -- mood which had come over Yeshu after Miriam's experience.

Jacob was not surprised by any of this. He knew Yeshu better than Yeshu knew himself. He shed tears for what he, Jacob, presumed his half-brother was going through. He agreed with Yehuda and Shimon that it was possible that Yeshu would deal with this horrible imbroglio with what today would be called manic and depressive shields. Jacob told the two that it was incumbent that they go down ("up" in another sense) to Jerusalem as soon as possible. Without explaining, Jacob rolled out his cart from the shed and had the horses pull all three of them back to Jerusalem. Jacob didn't have to explain; all of them KNEW in their hearts that they would not see Yeshu alive ever again.

When they arrived Jacob went straight to the quarters of Caiaphas. Jacob had never met him.

But he knew that Caiaphas was the key figure for getting the body back to the family for a proper burial. If you or I; or for that matter, Yehuda and Shimon --------------- we would all be escorted, rudely, off the premises. But Jacob had a quiet but commanding demeanor about him. The guards went back to Caiaphas and all three were welcomed into his somewhat lavish quarters. Caiaphas revealed to them at this very moment that Yeshu <i.e., Yeshu's body> was being cut down from the Roman Cross. A friend of Caiaphas who admired Yeshu from a distance had offered his own tomb for Yeshu's remains.

For the three half-brothers of Yeshu (but brothers to each other) it sank in. It was one thing to ride on a cart absent the dead body. But from this time forward it would the moment of truth.

Caiaphas had made the appropriate orders about the guards who were assigned to the tomb since it was not clear at all that some sort of hanky-panky would occur {{{after all it was just shy of a week wherein there was HUGE hanky-panky about two miles down the road}}}. After all that false "resurrection" -- one way or another -- was still in the air. Caiaphas made it his business that there simply would be none of that "resurrection" mania. Yes. Already the "Great *Shabbat*" had started. But Caiaphas understood what the brothers had to do trumped the *Halakha* on this matter. By eleven o-clock the three brothers loaded Yeshu's scared and wounded corpse onto the cart. Yehuda and Shimon opted to stay in Jerusalem and promised that they would come back to Nazareth in the near future.

The three brothers and Caiaphas chatted for a bit. Yehuda and Shimon took their leave. Jacob, then, decided that he would get on the road back to Nazareth. But Caiaphas persuaded Jacob to deal with what he, Caiaphas, deemed was a delicate, AND VERY IMPORTANT, matter. Tired as he was, Jacob nevertheless agreed to stay longer.

*****

LONG STORY SHORT:

"The Plan" hatched by Caiaphas and allowed by Pilate would have engaged Yeshu and El'azar in a scam whereby there would be a radical "upgrading" of the role of Yeshu's ministry. The conditions of the Roman Occupation had become SO onerous that more and more young Jewish men were attracted to Jerusalem which was rife with these ever-growing young Jewish men who generally were hell-bent on overthrowing the Roman Occupation. Caiaphas, early on, saw what was simmering. Caiaphas understood that if there were an insurrection Rome would crush it easily. But not only that. The very Polity of *Erets Yisrael* would be crushed. There is a huge difference between an Occupied Polity <in this case *Erets Yisrael*> with the Romans having all the power; OR, the Romans having all the power having utterly destroyed even a facsimile of Polity.

In effect -- Caiaphas was smart enough to see this possible and dreadful possibility was one wherein, at best, the Jews would have no Polity of their own; no standing of their own; a People without a country. Such an outcome might very well portend a scattering of the Jews; Jews without a country. Most certainly an occupied land -- horrible as it was -- without any Polity would morph into a Disapora.

Caiaphas's plan was a long shot.

The plan was to have centered on Yeshu. He was one of "them": the impoverished and disenfranchised. The "plan" was for one of their own <<Yeshu, but he now was dead>> to take on the mantle of the High Priest for the poor and

disenfranchised. In this Office <which would be set up by Caiaphas> "one of their own" would function as "The High Priest" for the poor and disenfranchised. As "High Priest of the poor and disenfranchised" this figure would be allowed an EXTRAORDINARY HONOR: *TO ENTER IN THE HOLY OF HOLIES OF THE TEMPLE ON YOM KIPPUR* **AND ARTICULATE ALOUD THREE TIMES THE SACRED NAME FROM *EXODUS*** 3:14.
But Yeshu was now dead.
Caiaphas now had the best choice of all: the beloved half-brother of Yeshu; a half-brother whose feet were firmly planted on the ground <a trait not shared by Yeshu>; a wise and even scholar of "The Laws and the Prophets." Likewise Jacob did not carry within himself a mercurial substrate which was characteristic of Yeshu. And finally, as a bonus, so to speak, one who dabbled lightly in the "magical" field but never to the extent of his half-brother. Caiaphas felt that this was the man for the job; indeed for the very continuance of the existence and well-being of *Erets Yisrael.*
Jacob agreed.
Of course Jacob would have to make arrangements back in Nazareth. And Caiaphas had to scrounge around for the kind of setting and building for this overall arrangement. It took a couple months or so, but a large and well-built edifice was built in the Western part of "Greater Jerusalem." It would not be a setting for Rabbis; it was not a *Beit haMidrash.* Rather a hide-out under the auspices of Jacob for the disenfranchised of good will and spirit. Jacob -- as was with the case of Yeshu -- was to concentrate on Scripture. Those who were from a background which, *halakhically,* included the Oral Torah orientation were welcomed on the condition that they deploy their Oral Torah practices quietly and, in any case, that they religiously adhered to

the *mitsvot* of Scripture (which was the practice of Yeshu himself). This 'retreat' was called "The Jerusalem Community."

By and large it worked; it worked for about three decades* But from its very foundation there were rumblings by other Jews to the effect that such a man of lowly pedigree would have such honors. Worse than that this Head of the Community had a background of an *am ha-ertes*. In the Summer of 62ce matters in Rome required that a large-enough contingent of Roman soldiers had to return to help out with the troubles in Rome. With this diminution of the Roman presence there were opportunities <so to speak> "to take matters into one's own hands." There was one figure who continually griped that a man whose background was an *am ha-erets* was allowed, on **YOM KIPPUR ITSELF**, to enter into the Holy of Holies of the Temple and articulate ALOUD three times the sacred NAME of God from *Exodus* 3:14.

This upstart organized a stoning. While Jacob was walking on the Temple Mount this gang stoned Jacob to death.

> *. {About five years after Yeshu died a guy showed up seeking admission to this "Jerusalem Community." His name was Saul/Paul. He was allowed to enter. His Jewish background was sparse. He was always grousing about the dietary *mitsvot*. There was much tension in the Community since this Saul/Paul was grousing all the time about the dietary *mitsvot*.
>
> Sad to say, Jacob was too lenient on this quasi Jew. Rather than kicking him out *tout suit* Jacob suggested that he, this Saul/Paul figure, become the "Apostle to the Gentiles."

This was a HUGE mistake on the part of Jacob. This Saul/Paul character was able to present himself as somehow tight with Yeshu by way of his thin relationship with Jacob, the half-brother, of Yeshu. He groused against all the dietary stipulations. Even worse, he suggested that Yeshu himself did not really care about the dietary stipulations. In other words he was ignorant or lying.
Saul/Paul bandied around what he called his close spiritual kinship with Jacob when in fact -- and he knew it -- they couldn't stand each other.
Long story short: he came to hate the restrictions which Jacob eventually insisted upon. But his worst "achievement" was his creation of a "Yeshu" in the image and likeness **<u>OF HIMSELF</u>** in his "Letters." His Letters were the seeds of Anti-Semitism. Saul/Paul was popular with the self-ordained "Fathers of the Church." ***<u>UGH!</u>***}

****
****
****
****
****
****

<u>PART THREE.</u>
EL'AZAR POST YESHU.

THE DAY AFTER.
El'azar

Coming Home.

His own parents gave him the cold shoulder. They wouldn't mention the name "Yeshu." And largely they didn't talk to El'azar.

Miriam was worse. She never cried. She never showed any emotion at all. She was Zombi-esque. She did not greet anyone or respond to a greeting. She had lost much weight; it was frightening. She finally died about six months later. And she had never spoken of Yeshu again.

As for El'azar he was largely shunned; even shunned by Miriam.

What was worse for El'azar was the way Yeshu comported himself in those last two and a-half days. It was a totally different Yeshu who in fact-- albeit he did not inform anyone -- had made a determination to die in such a way that no-one <especially *El'azar*> would be ruined. Had he not been hell bent to die would he have maintained that original and planned total re-make? No-one will ever know. But how could anyone like Yeshu continue the way he did continue in those last two and a half days?

The answer, however, is simple: i). Yeshu WANTED to die after the stupid "plan" brought Miriam down to a state from which she would never recover; and, ii). given that, he wanted to comport himself such that he would (except for Miriam who would never recover) be the only one to take the "hit" for the stupid "plan."

The family was indeed stunned by the whole ridiculous scam. But slowly -- excepting Miriam -- the entrenched realities and necessities of living prevailed.

Miriam ate almost nothing. She wasn't trying to not eat; it was just that she could not eat. One night -- sometime after the crucifixion -- when Miriam did not come out of her bedroom her mother came into her room. Was she sleeping? She put her hand on Miriam's forehead. It was cold. She had died. She was buried in the crypt wherein El'azar had lived for four days.

Everything seemed depressing to El'azar. He tried to remember the good times with Yeshu; but it didn't work; the so-called "good times" were, in the final analysis, rather surfacey.
*****
It was hard to keep abreast with time for El'azar; he was now in, so to speak, in an alternate universe. He wanted desperately to leave the family for what he, El'azar, had done in concert with Yeshu (and in concert with the "Plan" hatched by Caiaphas). His family, by this time, were as kind as they could be. But he felt doomed all the time.
Then one fine day he found out that Yeshu's brother Jacob had become the minister, so to speak, of what might be called a "Retreat House." For the first time since the whole mess transpired, there was some hope in El'azar's demeanor. Without alerting his parents he checked things out on his own and even got a warm welcoming from Jacob. They talked for two hours straight. Jacob suggested that he spend some time in this "retreat" (so to speak).
*****

When El'azar brought up his intention to move over for a couple of months to the "Jerusalem Community" his father went ballistic. He was remanded to his bedroom; he would eat in his bedroom; and if he had to have some exercise outside such could only do so when accompanied by a servant to the father. He was a prisoner in his own home.
El'azar could not live this way. Secretly he packed a bag of clothes and left the homestead. He

waited until his father's servant was taking a bowel movement and he got out of the house by the window. He walked the long distance all the way to the OTHER side of Jerusalem.

He knocked on the door and it was Jacob who let him in. Jacob was glad that this young man had found his way to this "Jerusalem Community." Jacob was happy to hear his story. He was invited to stay for as long as he wanted.

After a few days Jacob suggested a project for El'azar. Why not tell the whole story -- the good, the bad, and the ugly -- about his companionship with Yeshu. Jacob had immediately understood that this would be the best thing for him. And it was. It took a long time; but it was worth it.

However, towards the end of this project there was a HUGE downside. His father was now totally disgusted with him. First it was that nonsense centered on Yeshu <<the father quietly downplaying HIS OWN welcoming of Yeshu back before the fraud "Resurrection">>; his son should have known better. And now his son was staying with that half-brother of Yeshu. That sealed it. El'azar was taken out of the Will.

El'azar stayed in that retreat home until he had finished his project. He gave himself credit for his honest accounting of that intense time with Yeshu. Again: the good; the bad; and the ugly. The whole thing was cathartic for El'azar.

The finishing of his long project had the effect of NO LONGER wanting to stay at Jacob's Retreat. Spending this time with Jacob was now becoming slim. The catharsis which El'azar achieved by writing that account of Yeshu <the good, the bad; the ugly> opened his eyes to the shallowness of Yeshu's ministry (excepting, of course, the rather noble way he comported himself <centered on how

devastating the fraud was for Miriam> for last six days of his life).

Yeshu died nobly but one could not, in fairness, maintain that his ministry was always beneficial for others; largely a mixed bag. The reality is that the Preacher did much good and, equally, perpetrated much evil albeit he did not aim for such an outcome. Prior to the fraud "resurrection" Yeshu tended not to see the downside for others by virtue of his ministry.

ENOUGH!!!

*****

El'azar had to admit it. His time in this Jerusalem Community was very beneficial. Partly by the support <both material and spiritual> by way of Jacob. But far, far, more important was the catharsis he gained by writing that "good/bad/ugly" account of Yeshu and how El'azar himself comported his life back then in the mode of "good/bad/ugly."

But the "bottom-line" was clear. He did not know how he would turn out over time. In any case he had to get out of this place. He certainly could not go back to his homestead. El'azar had a psyche which precluded suicide. Funds were almost nothing. In any case he had to get out of this "Jerusalem Community" here even if he had to become a beggar in Jerusalem. And, in fact that is just what he did.

*****

It was not long before all of this filtered back to his father. A rich and powerful man such as El'azar's father gets to find out EVERYTHING.

His father was smart enough not to chase his son down who would only refuse to go back to the homestead. So he contacted the young and new Head Rabbi in Jerusalem: Rabbi Yochanan ben

Tsakkai. He was the Head of the *Pharisaically*-oriented Beit ha-Midrash in Jerusalem; in effect, it was, so to speak, the Flagship *Beit haMidrash* for all of Jerusalem.

Rabbi Yochanan sent students into the back alleys of Jerusalem to track down El'azar. El'azar was discovered. Tsakkai himself went to meet with him after his students had come back with the information.

El'azar -- who never had an overweight problem -- was fifteen pounds lower than his normal weight. El'azar initially refused an invitation to go and live in Tsakkai's roomy *Beit ha Midrash* in Jerusalem. Tsakkai was savvy. This was a young man who had not eaten a decent meal in three weeks. Tsakkai just said to him: *have it your way.* He turned around and started back to the Shul. It was only a matter of seconds, not minutes, before this hungry young man acquiesced to this Rabbi.

Everybody knows the story after this. El'azar (who already had significant training in Jewish Studies by way of tutors hired by El'azar's father) became in a matter of just six intense months the most subtle and most accurate *halakhist* in this flagship *Beit haMidrash* in Jerusalem. Rabbi Yochanan T-sakkai had carefully checked the progress of this gifted young man.

Of course T-sakkai and El'azar's father were in cahoots with each other. T-sakkai informed the father of El'azar that this halakhic genius would be, so to speak, the *magister ludi* for a certain session of that flagship *Beit ha Midrash*. Tsakkai made sure that the father would stand in the last row so that his son would not notice him.

Everything went well that day. El'azar was stupendous in his presentation and orchestration of the argumentation. He was an instant star. And the son's eyes welled up when he saw his father.

He was back in the fold <and his patrimony was re-instated>.

****
****
****
****
****
****
****
****

Fast Forward:
the whys and wherefores of "the day of the coiled snake"

Let us take a pause to celebrate the special and difficult exertion on the part of El'azar with respect to the fashioning of this special oven.

Average Jews with low income could barely acquire an oven. But ovens -- as they were available at that time -- were very costly. But that's not the worst of it.

Small creatures -- like a *sherets* for instance -- are endemically *tamei* which means it can easily transfer *tumah*. With most ovens at that time and place, if a *sherets* -- dead or alive -- falls into one of those ovens ***the whole oven is rendered* tamei** with the consequence that the oven must be shattered and buried. Obviously such occurrences were common. And this unhappy situation carried with it that the cost of the *tamei-ed* oven (which would have to be then shattered and buried) with the consequence that the family had to get along without an oven.

The rich had less to worry about. But the burden on the poor would be ***immense***.

El'azar -- one who had the wherewithal -- could replace a shattered *tamei-ed* oven. But he believed that the burden of the poor was immense ***and unfair***.

El'azar brought his talents to meliorate this horrible situation for the poor especially. He put much ingenuity (and MUCH energy and time) to craft a certain kind of oven which would *minimize* the *tumah* which would be transferred. The intricate way by which El'azar crafted his special oven was such that the *tumah* transferred is minimal. Because of the ring-like threads of sand in the composition of this special kind of oven the conTAMination would not spread; it would be *tamei* ONLY to the section of the oven which came in direct contact with the *sherets* <or some other such-like pest>. The spread of *tumah* was limited to that contact.

And keep this in mind:

Talmudic experts then and now are all in agreement that INDEED the kind of oven crafted by El'azar could, relatively easily in most cases, be maintained **tahor** ***such that even if something like a sherets falling into the oven the 'tameied' contact involved would be minimal by virtue of the intricate casting of this oven. Given this intricate craftsmanship of El'azar's special oven the only area which would be ---- for most situations --*** **"tameied"** ***would be limited to the contact of, say, a sherets falling into the oven; it would be a very small contact leaving the rest of the oven unaffected.***

The clever intricacy involved radically limiting any passing on of **tumah** ***to the rest of the oven. The relatively small area of*** **tumah** ***could be exhumed from the oven without transmitting*** **tumah** ***to the rest of the oven. The rest of the oven remained uncontaminated. No need, then, for breaking up the whole oven and burying it***

****
****
****

But Joshua and Aqiba were hell-bent to *WIN** on a matter totally extraneous to the matter of the true discussion under review. Their agendum had little to do with the oven *per se*. Goading El'azar (who in his later years had acquired a mercurial orientation when challenged) to such an extent that his mercurial way of defending the *tahor* status of the oven was **such** that the majority turned on him quite apart from the final adjudication of the matter (i.e., whether or not the proposed oven could be rendered *tahor* with only a minor adjustment to the area which was rendered *tamei*.) Shame on Rabbi Joshua; Shame on Rabbi Aqiba; they goaded Rabbi El'azar/Eliezer into his mercurial antics (which, of course, did not sit well with the Rabbis in attendance..
****

The Yavne Community was destined, so to speak, to break asunder within the *Beit haMidrah*. Most of the scholars were from the Pharisaic Sect. This means that the majority faction <the Pharisees> counted the invention called "The Oral Torah" <<an ever-bulging set of *halakhot* over the years and even centuries>> as part of the *Halakha which somehow or another?* were "received"* *from the mouth of Moishe at Sinai*!!!!!
*****
The Pharisees loved their self-invented <u>*halakhot*</u>. Indeed these *halakhot* of the Pharisaic Sect tended to be honored in such a way that in practice (but not in theory) their treasured *halakhot* are honored as equal to the *mitsvot* of Scripture (if not MORE in most cases) by the Pharisaic Sect.

*. {It was the Pharisaic invention that in addition to the written *mitsvot* from Moishe at Sinai there were also a whole raft of mandates <*halakhot*>* "received" by the Pharisaic Sect allegedly from Moishe. *But* ***miraculously****! The flow of additions upon additions of* halakhot *over the years and centuries continued long after Moishe died!* How interesting!!!!! AND, **<u>how convenient</u>** that their *minhaggim* had miraculously somehow 'graduated' to sacred *halakhot*. And somehow *these halakhot were also initiated at the time of Moishe!!!!! and somehow, after Moise's death, were still coming right on up to and unto of the Hasmonean Period!*
WOW!
**. {{I'm not the *dufus* which you take me to be. You probably think that this *goy-boy amateur* is confusing genuine *halakhot* with something like "Rabbinic Enactments" and, later, under the rubric of *takanot*. But that is not the case. To be sure there were always those <<e.g., the Scripture-centric *Soferim*>> whose assignments were to facilitate the deployment of the functional requirements which had to be deployed such that ---------- *will miracles never cease?* ------- the *mitsvot* of Scripture, initially and to be sure. But then and later, there was *<u>the very debatable</u>* putative *halakhot* which kept on streaming from the mouth of Moishe (over the centuries somehow) before he died and which --- *glory be to God!!!!* had to be facilitated even though Moishe was dead. Nor did the flow stop. Again! -- miracle of miracles! -- even MORE *halakhot* somehow were transmitted

centuries from Sinai! Will miracles never cease?! But they could not come from Moishe since Moishe was long dead by this time. Who, then, was transmitting these new *halakhot*?
Shhhhh! QUIET! Don't' rock the boat!
Again I am not confusing this uncanny flow of putative *halakhot* centuries after the Sinai episode with "Rabbinic Enactments" [or, if you will, *takanot*] which are deployed to facilitate the deployment of the *mitsvot* ((no problem there; they were written down in Scripture)) and, as well the *halakhot* which, it is claimed, had an Oral genesis via Moishe (and some would say via Joshua as well). And **long** after Moishe and Joshua died ---- ***somehow or other!*** ----- new *halakhot* <<out of the thin air>> kept springing up without there being a Moishe (or a Joshua). Miracles!
As we have seen, as time went on more proliferating of *halakhot* continued to spring up from the Pharisaic Sect.* These "new" *halakhot*? Were these from Moishe as well **even though he had died centuries ago????** And isn't it amazing that many of these "new" halakhot were -- most curiously -- the favored minhaggim of the Pharisaic Sect??? hmmmmmmm.
How chummy!
In any case Rabbinic Enactments are not *halakhot*.}}

About these new *halakhot*.
Who was promulgating these "heaps and heaps" of Oral Torah *halakhot* ? Was it Moishe speaking from his grave? Was it Joshua <i.e., the Joshua back in the Promised Land> from his grave? Maybe;

maybe not. But this Pharisaic fixation couldn't help itself. The prolific stream of *halakhot* from Moishe **somehow!!!** kept rolling along **for centuries**. Suspiciously, it is to be noted that many of the treasured minhaggim of the Pharisaic Sect were being, one way or another "received" (somehow) as genuine *halakhot*. Let that sink in.

****
****
****

And then there is this:
It was a MOST REVERED mandate in the Pharisaic Sect that Oral Torah *halakhot* were **NEVER, NEVER, NEVER** to be put into writing. But the Sect which invented the Oral Torah to begin with, ***by golly!, found a verse in Psalms*** (with ambiguous syntax to boot)**!!!!!** ***which was portrayed by Rabbi Aqiba as Scriptural validation for OVERTURNING the sacred mandate that NEVER!; NEVER!; NEVER!; were Oral Torah*** **halakhot** ***would be committed to writing***.
This matter has "bad faith" written all over it.
Let's take a look.

i). The Verse in question is *Psalms* 119:126.
There is, syntactically, an ambiguity which allows "Hashem" to be construed either as the actor of the first part of this verse; or as the recipient of this part of the verse.
But when the syntax involved is joined with the semantical underpinning of this verse as a whole, it becomes clear that the "Hashem" of the verse is not the actor of this verse. Rather, the "Hashem" of the verse is the recipient.
ii). Accordingly we can put forth the "plain sense" of this verse as the following:

For it is a time to act for Hashem: they have voided your Torah.

iii). Keep in mind that the verse is being deployed by Rabbi Aqiba at the time when the Pharisaic Sect at Yavne had finally succeeded in gaining control of the Yavne Community as a whole. The import of this is huge. The Yavne Community, in its *Beit haMidrash*, had set in motion from its beginning a Scripture-centric <and only Scripture-centric> for the determining of the *Halakha*. For the first two decades (roughly) this was the only way for determining the *Halakha* which was being allowed at Yavne.

This foundational basis was operative for almost two decades at Yavne. This foundational basis was deeply resented by the Pharisaic Sect at Yavne insofar as this foundational set-up eschewed the Pharisaic invention of the "Oral Torah."

Certain developments -- including especially the back-to-back deaths of Rabbi Elisha ben Abuya's two sons -- conspired to bring the beginnings of a revolution at Yavne. And it is this at juncture that the leaders of the Pharisaic Sect (((Rabbis Joshua, Aqiba, and the young Shimon bar Yokhai)))* "flexed their muscles" and took over the leadership of the Yavne Community. The original leadership ----- Rabban; Rabbi Elisha ben Abuya; and, a bit later, Rabbi El'azar ben Hurcanus ----- were deposed one way or another-----:

Rabban was deposed <<in a shameful manner by Rabbis Joshua and Aqiba>> by the Pharisaic majority because he had thrown his weight to this "New Beginning" centered around the determining the *Halakha* in a Scripture-centric manner and ONLY as a Scripture-centric manner.

*. [[[[The young Shimon bar Yokhai was thrilled to be brought into the higher strata of the Pharisaic faction at Yavne. ((((((((He

would not receive his Rabbinate until right on the dangerous cusp of the *Bar Kochba* Revolt.))))))))) This was the time when Rabbis Joshua and Aqiba were going about the business of overturning the original protocols by which the Yavne Community was founded. Joshua and Aqiba delegated Shimon bar Yokhai to do some of the "dirty-work" in overthrowing the foundational figures and protocols of the Yavne Community's birthing.

And later on ((i.e., after the *Putsch* of 94)) our Shimon bar Yokhai joined with Rabbi Aqiba in the launching of "THE SECOND" (aka: The MISHNAH). Over time, the Mishna included many facets; indeed many facets which were extraneous to the "cataloguing" of the Oral Torah *halakhot*. Prior to the *Putsch* of 93/94ce there was no cataloguing of those putative Oral Torah *halakhot*. The immediate reaction to the *Putsch* was to have a document given over to a cataloguing of Oral Torah *halakhot*. However, with the passage of time this MISHNA ("THE SECOND") addressed many other matters as well and in some detail as well. <<Indeed, this "SECOND" kept on generating a huge array of matters other than creating a home for Oral Torah *halakhot*. It would be a little more than a century before the MISHNA had its final redaction under the auspices of Rabbi Judah.

Take note of the following:

There was a HUGE **AND SACRED** impediment for even ***having at all*** any writing down or cataloguing of Oral Torah *halakhot*. Indeed, doing such would be to destroy the first principle of there being Oral Torah AT ALL. **YET, the original animus at Yavne----- post *COUP* ----- was to allow the Oral Torah *halakhot* to be transcribed in writing**. As we have seen this was a gross violation of the Oral Torah whose highest mandate was that Oral Torah *halakhot* would ***NEVER/EVER*** commit Oral Torah *halakhot* to be put in written form.

But with Rabbi Aqiba at the helm <in reality, but not in theory> "***anything goes.***" As we shall see below, he scrounged around Scripture looking for **some** -- however skimpy -- validation **FOR VIOLATING THE SACRED MANDATE OF THE ORAL TORAH TO THE EFFECT THAT *NEVER, NEVER, NEVER*** would be committed to writing. Accordingly, then: *Psalms* 119:126.

***** ***** *****

The "Architecture" of the MISHNA was orchestrated by Rabbi Aqiba: First the "Six Sederim" and then, within the schema of the Six Sederim, the forty-eight Chapters dispersed over those Six Sederim. Predictably, Rabbi Aqiba tired of the project which he had launched. He brought in Shimon to continue the project. Rabbi Aqiba was an "excitement-junkie." He tired of the onerous work of launching "The Second." He bequeathed this onerous task to Simon who continued the Project. It was Shimon bar Yokhai who ended up doing the heavy lifting in launching the MISHNA

****

****

****

In the diabolical run-up to the "Bar Kochba Revolt" (promoted assiduously by Rabbi Aqiba) a group of five "pre-Rabbis" <including Shimon bar Yokhai and Meir> achieved their Rabbinate status on the cusp of that War which should never have been engaged. Rabbi Aqiba's terrible support of that nefarious "Son of a Star" almost ruined forever the Rabbinate Itself.
The fallout of the War ----- which never should have been engaged but was engaged by virtue of Aqiba's infatuation with that "Son of a Star" -- was horrendous. "Rivers of Jewish blood" were the price for Aqiba's fatuous support (i.e., bringing about the Rabbinate to support the Rebellion) of a foolish "Son of a Star."
And let us not forget. Having been decimated in that **second !!!!!** War with Rome, there were **additional** "rivers of blood" by virtue of the long-lived Hadrianic Repression. SHAME! A war which never should have been engaged **AT ALL**.
Largely because of Aqiba's machinations which put the Rabbinic Movement behind that "Son of a Star" Rabbi Shimon bar Yokhai, (correctly, I aver) generated a powerful hatred for his one-time mentor. Rivers of Jewish Blood. He and his son had had to hideout **for twelve years** by virtue of the Hadrianic Repression.]

****
****
****

The case against Rabbi Elisha ben Abuya <<he was in fact the first to be deposed>> is complex. Most certainly the deaths of his two sons affected his whole demeanor. When he returned to the *Beit ha Midrash* he seemed to have regained his spirit as is indicated by his first opening gambit. <<<<<<<Confer page 486 of the Lauterbach translation of Tractate *Kaspa* contained in volume two of the *Mekhilta*.>>>>>>> However, he was not supported even by his two closest mentees, Rabbi Josiah and Rabbi Jonathan.

In turn Rabbi Aqiba was motivated to take advantage of this significant lack of support. Rabbi Elisha ben Abuya suffered a significant "loss of face" for the returning Head of the *Beit haMidrash.* [Confer from the bottom of page 486 right through the end of Tractate *KASPA* page 492; ***THE DAY THE MUSIC DIED***.]

When the second session convened, [from the first full paragraph on page 488]* Rabbi Aqiba challenged in a staccato fashion all of the offerings put forth by Elisha who, in turn <contrary to his normal demeanor> replied in a more strident staccato manner. To be sure, Elisha's counter offerings were valid. But the mood in the room had changed.

Who knows? Was it the very mysterious back-to-back deaths of his sons? The fact that he was not getting support from his usual allies? And, perhaps most saliently, he had been "beaten-down" by the loss of his sons. Even as Elisha was putting forth the correct adjudications, they were not sustained. <<Prior to this session Rabbi Elisha had NEVER been overturned in an adjudication.>>

He became verbally aggressive. And he 'lost-face" by virtue of such aggression. (((The reader at this point is suggested to visit the dramatic pages from 488 through 492 in volume-ii of the *Mekhilta* <<wherein you will find the "dramatic Seven NOes." **The Day the Music died**.)))

Rabbi Elisha had lost "face," big time. He stepped down as Head of the *Beit ha Midrash*. He had the right to name a successor. He named El'azar ben Hurcanus.>>>>>>>
****
****
iv). Continuing on:

For it is a time to act for Hashem: they have voided your Torah.

Psalms 119:126.
Let's be clear. After the deposing (-- one way or another --) of Rabban, second; Rabbi Elisha, first; and, finally, El'azar ben Hurcanus, third, the power went fully to the Pharisaic Sect. For all practical purposes, it was Rabbis Aqiba and Joshua (along with Aqiba's mentee, Shimon bar Yokhai) who had the power.
v). THE MISHNAH: "The SECOND."
Aqiba took it upon himself to launch "The Second." He worked hard on it for a number of years. But then he tired of it and left it to others. The truth was that he lost interest in the project. He more or less retired. (((Later on Aqiba's juices came back to him by becoming enchanted with that scum-bag, "The Son of the Star!" And there was, this time, no Caiaphas who could siphon off Revolutionary dreams. Rabbi Aqiba fiercely [and largely successfully] lobbied the major Rabbis at Yavne and elsewhere to put the Rabbinic Movement behind this "Son of a Star.")))
Doing such was a disaster. In effect that "Bar Kochba War" (in sync with the subsequent Hadrianic Repression) effectively terminated *Erets Yisrael* as a country as a Polity.
It is one thing for one's country to be Occupied; the Occupation would eventually recede and *Erets Yisrael* -- and its Polity -- would be eventually re-constituted. You might recall that, back

then, -- when the matter was Yeshu -- Caiaphas counseled just that.
In any case, short-sighted minds jumped on the bandwagon of that "Son of a Star." It led to the utter decimation of *Erets YIsrael* as a Polity. This was the beginning of the Great and Horrible Diaspora.
God put forth one last opportunity: The events of 1947/1948 and 1967. But this is the last chance. And if *Beit Yisrael* should disappear from History-- for one reason and/or another -- soon after all of Humanity will disappear from History.

vi). ------ *GOD IS GLORIOUS, NO!?* -------
PSALMS 119:126. As we shall see below, this verse -- taken out of context -- is the verse, found by Aqiba, which ----- putatively ----- functioned as Scriptural validation for doing what the Oral Torah orientation did best: **the proliferation of *halakhot***. There is something deeply curious in this citation from Scripture <*Psalms* 119:126>. To be sure, when the Pharisaic Sect invented the Oral Torah they did not bother for Scriptural validation. Fast forward a few centuries. Now ((we are in Yavne soon after the Pharisaic *Putsch* of 94ce)) all of a sudden, and after centuries of inventing Oral Torah *halakhot* of the Pharisaic Sect (-- and now in control of the Yavne Community --) NOW ALL OF A SUDDEN the Pharasaic Sect feels the need to justify this move whereby the Oral Torah must, so to speak, validate itself by Scripture. [[[The dynamic has always been legion although it didn't have a heading until Freud created the vocabulary of something deeply disturbing: *The sons killing the Father.* The leaders of the Pharisaic *Coup* orchestrated the "killing" <i.e., "deposing"> of the ruling 'Troika' to wit: -- Rabbis Elisha ben Abuya <who was the Head of the *Beit ha Midrash* at Yavne>; <Rabban <who was

the Head of the Yavne Community as a whole>; <and the gifted "turncoat" Rabbi El'azar Hurcanus who succeeded Rabbi Elisha as Head of the *Beit haMidrash* only <and quickly> to be deposed in his turn.]]]

*****

In any case this Scriptural "fig-leaf" {i.e., *Psalms 119:126*] was just a veneer of justification. And that's all they needed having ignominiously dispatched the ruling "Troika."

But this move predicated on a spurious reading of a verse in Scripture -- which as we shall see below -- GROSSLY **VIOLATED** the *original and foundational sacred mandate* ***OF THE ORAL TORAH ITSELF!!!!!*** What a tawdry way to get their way. Shame on the Pharisaic Sect.

Pause so as to get a sense of what really is going on. Consider: the foundational principle of the Oral Torah was to the effect that ***NEVER; NEVER; NEVER*** will Oral Torah *halakhot* be committed to writing. But guess what? This sacred mandate will, from now on, be **VIOLATED BY THEIR OWN SECT WHICH NOW WILL BE COMMITTED TO WRITING NEW *HALAKHOT*!!!!** using, as we shall see, verse 119:126 of Guilty feelings, revealingly, indict themselves. To assuage these feelings the leaders of the Pharisaic faction <<at this point Rabbis Joshua, Aqiba, and the young Shimon bar Yokhai>> had pulled out of thin air the notion that a Scriptural verse <it will be *Psalms* 119:126> will function as a 'fig-leaf' for what they are doing. YET, they were **violating their own and most fundamental principle: *NEVER! NEVER! NEVER! are Oral Torah* Halakhot *to be consigned to writing!!!!*** <<<<and, furthermore, the correct reading of *Psalms* 119:129, in the final analysis,

does NOT validate this GROSS **VIOLATION** of the Oral Torah.>>>
*****

YES! OF COURSE! The Sect was hell-bent to put for Itself a "SECOND" Scripture <in a manner of speaking>. It wants "this SECOND" be, in effect <albeit not saying it in so many words>, as it were, an alternate Scripture. The critical moment was at Yavne when the *PUTSCH* of 94ce gave them control of the *Beit ha Midrash* by excommunicating "the last man standing" <this will have been the ex-communication of Rabbi El'azar>. And Yavne, at this time, was the "flagship" community for *Beit Yisrael*. At this point in Judaism, the caveats of Yavne were going to be the caveats of Judaism. <<Note that this flagship community will <later on> disappear, of course, by virtue of Aqiba's grossly foolish worshipping of that "Son of a Star.">>
****
****
****

Again: The SECOND. Aqiba's baby. But then he got bored with it. Later on, as we shall see, this Rabbi -- who was at one time was enthused by Yeshu even though he never met Yeshu in the flesh -- was getting bored. Now bored with his work on THE SECOND he looked around for more exciting venues. By this time, even Rabbi Joshua understood that Rabbi Aqiba was but a "narcissist."* Rabbi Joshua no longer wanted to be in Aqiba's presence. Joshua died before the ruminations of that "Son of a Star" changed Aqiba into a monster.

*. OF COURSE that word itself was not deployed <albeit "Narcissus" had been around for centuries>. In any case Rabbi Aqiba was a narcissist.
****
****

Rabbi Aqiba was famous for bending the meaning of words; weighting the *minutiae* of Scripture so as to violate the "plain sense" of Scripture; always looking for oralizations of words in the service of changing the obvious meaning of the words in question. In his heart --- (and in his actual practice) --- he had taken his clue from his first mentor, Gum-zu.

It is more than interesting that the Pharisaic Sect -- following the leadership of Rabbi Aqiba on this matter -- allowed the verse, *Psalms* 119:126 to be construed as **validating** the gross twisting of the verse so as to allow the contradiction that was *NEVER! NEVER! NEVER!* to be committed to writing was, miraculously, **by a tortured reading of the verse in question**, ended with this <in effect>: *WELL GUYS IT IS REALLY OK TO* ***VIOLATE*** *--- ONE WAY OR ANOTHER, BY GOD --- THE MOST SACRED MANDATE OF THE ORAL TORAH ORIENTATION.* Mauling the verse <<<<*Psalms* 119:126 {which has some syntactical ambiguity about it >>>> in question to suit the ORAL TORAH enthusiasts. The verse in question from *Psalms* – with its two ways of being understood -- turns out that **NEITHER** of its two meanings involved in this 119:126 of *Psalms* supports the ENORMOUS *chutzpah* of **VIOLATING** the original ruling caveat of the Oral Torah to begin with.

But this is the very essence of Rabbi Aqiba's attitude to Scripture. Leadership such as that brings on a roguish regimen. This Aqibian juggling which cannot be juggled --- believe it or not! -- became by extension over the centuries, the group validation of most Orthodox Rabbis in our time who dote on Rabbi Aqiba and the Oral Torah orientation. Long-lastliness does not always indicate great achievement. Indeed, what has been going on in *Beit Yisrael* for about eighteen and a half centuries, is simply a long sojourn in the wilderness. Longevity does not, of itself, produce good outcomes. *Beit Yisrael* is all too comfortable with mediocrity (**AT BEST**). I aver that what is bequeathed from "generation unto generation" for *Beit Yisrael* is a sparse shadow. *Beit Yisrael* is like the KING'S WARROBE. For the KING is wearing nothing at all. It's embarrassing. And it cannot continue this way. *Beit Yisrael* may be more close to extinction than one might think. And there is only one exit from this dead-end:

<u>**SHUVU!**</u>
O MY BACKSLIDING CHILDREN
except Akher
<he never left>

SHAME!
*****

It can't go on like this. For *Beit Yisrael* time is running short. There are, in the final analysis, just too outcomes (in our time). One option is to keep on going the way things have been going mesmerized and blind. This would eventually become a death spiral. Yes, it is true that the horrific leaders of Iran who viciously hate Jews might attempt to virtually annihilate most of the population of *Erets Yisrael*. But my sense of it is that the leaders of *Erets Yisrael* will do whatever it takes to thwart the hateful rulers of present-day Iran. The real danger, then, is the one which we don't see as a danger. And what is that? Very simple. Being and becoming blind to what is happening ***within*** *Beit Yisrael*. And what IS happening? "the same-old same-old." That is the true danger; that is a death spiral for *Beit Yisrael*.
Is there any hope then? Yes:

ACCORDINGLY, CHOOSE LIFE!

A how do we do it?
It has always been with us since the time of *Jeremiah* 3:14:

SHUVU*!*
O MY BACKSLIDING CHILDREN

Think about it: *If nothing changes nothing changes.*

***** ***** ***** ***** *****

***** ***** *****

***** ***** ***** ***** *****

****

****

****

Back to Yavne. What Yavne orchestrated for those initial and almost twenty-years is the goal for our own time if we are brave enough <<if we stop slumbering and calling it "religion">> to *re-instatee that beautiful status quo ante at Yavne*.
There was, back in the day, a coterie of Scholars <<a coterie much much fewer than the numbers of Pharisees>> of the very highest order. This tight coterie (which came to include "star" members of the Pharisaic Sect who had jettisoned <at least publically> the validity of the Oral Torah invention>. The major players were constituted by a curious set of figures:
First and foremost was Nekhunya ben Qana* from the Priesthood who -- along with Rabbi Yochanan ben Tsakkai who was a Pharisee (and certainly not a Priest). In addition there was the majorly young genius and as well, the pride and joy of Nekhunya in these affairs: "Rabbi Elisha ben Abuya." All of this was straight out from the beginning.

*. ["Rabbi" Nekhunya ben Qana was rather advanced in age when he came to Yavne. As mentioned above he mentored the gifted "Elisha ben Abuya" in the ins and outs of the HA-KATUV (i.e., Scripture-centric) orientation. Rabbi Nekhunya (the former Priest prior to the destruction of the Temple) died circa 75ce. He could die in peace knowing that his star mentee -- Elisha -- would function as the Head of the *Beit ha Midrash* at Yavne.

**. [Shortly after the *Beit haMidrash* came into play at Yavne ---------[[[keep in mind that in the early years at Yavne (say, approximately, 70 on up to 73/74, the members of this Yavne Community were engaged in helping and dealing with the many refugees who were refugees by virtue of the War with Rome along with the destruction of the Temple]]] ------- there emerged a Rabbi named "El'azar ben Hurcanus" who hailed from the Pharisaic faction at Yavne. This well-educated figure came to appreciate the Scripture Centric <and ONLY Scripture Centric> manner of determining the *Halakha* as put forth by "Rabbi Elisha ben Abuya" (((later, due to deep circumstances, this Rabbi would come to be referred to as "Rabbi Ishmael ben Elisha"))). Rabbi Elisha eventually came to mentor Rabbi El'azar. This figure from Bethany came to be quite adept in this "New Beginning" wherein the determining of the *Halakha* was predicated on Scripture-centricity and ONLY Scirpture-centricity. In effect this Rabbi El'azar came to join with Rabban and Rabbi Elisha ben Abuya in forming a "Troika" by which the Yavne Community would be governed.*

*. <<Of course -------- El'azar **was** a star member of the *Pharisaically-oriented Beit haMidrash* run by Rabban in Jerusalem -------- it was automatic on the part of the Pharisaical leaders (Rabbis Joshua; Rabbi Aqiba; and the young Shimon bar Yokhai) that El'azar would be understood by his Pharisaic "colleagues" as a "Turncoat." So too for Rabban.>>

]

Accordingly <and again> these three honored figures were the foundation stones of this "NEW BEGINNING" predicated on "Scripture-Centricity" {and ONLY "Scripture Centricity"} whether it be the interpretation of the narratives of Scripture and/or the proper interpretation of the *mitsvot* of Scripture. ((Please keep in mind: Nekhunya ben Qana, set in motion of the Scripture-centric -- and only Scripture-centricity -- for the determining of the true Halakha. He died less than five years from the foundation of the Yavne Community at 70ce. Nekhunya had, for a long time <back when there was a Temple> trained the gifted "Rabbi Elisha ben Abuya" to be able to take over being the Head of the sessions of the *Beit ha-Midrash* at Yavne.))
So, as the real beginning of the *Beit haMidrash* circa 75ce was set in motion -------- (((the upheaval of the destruction of the Temple (and the war associated with it) the community was deeply involved with dealing with refugees from that horrific War and Its outcome in the years from 70 to about 74))) -------- it was Rabbi Elisha ben Abuya who became the Head of the *Beit ha Midrash*.
These founders -- Rabban,** the Head of the whole Community; and then, Rabbi Elisha ben

Elisha, primarily; and Rabbi El'azar-ben Hurcanus, secondarily;*** -- constituted the leadership of the sessions of the *Beit ha Midrash* at Yavne. The understanding was that in matters of the *Halakha* all would be determined according to Scripture-centricity and ONLY Scripture-centricity. Indeed, for almost two decades this was the sacred norm for determining the *Halakha.*

The whole point of this is to the effect that -- given the horror of the destruction of the Second Temple and the HUGE disaster of that War with Rome -- it was requisite for *Beit Yisrael* to birth a NEW BEGINNING for *Beit Yisrael.*

Rabban was Head of the whole Community at Yavne and the young and exceptionally-gifted Rabbi Elisha ben Abuya was the appointed Head of the *Beit haMidrash* at Yavne. Soon after, a third figure (noted above) joined the Leadership of *Beit haMidrash* at Yavne: "Rabbi El'azar ben Hurcanus." Rabban had had him as a student in his flagship Beit ha Midrash in Jerusalem. Back then both Rabban (and therefore El'azar ben Hurcanus) were immersed --- in the Oral Torah orientation.

But the War and the destruction of the Second Temple changed everything (at least for a couple of decades).

Rabbi El'azar, soon after the founding of the Yavne Community ----- and even though he was not **initially** part of the group which understood that a "new beginning" was requisite ----- came to understand that this "new beginning" would have to be founded on principles which were ***definitely not normative*** for the Pharisaic Sect. El'azar understood that there cannot BE a "new beginning' unless the old <<<i.e., the preponderance of the members of the Pharisaic Sect committed {in their hearts, if not in theory} to the Oral Torah orientation>>> was put to rest. Yes, El'azar's status

as "Rabbi" was earned in the Beit haMidrash led by Rabban <wherein the Oral Torah orientation was normative>. But El'azar, now stationed at Yavne, came to realize that Elisha ben Abuya was more learn'ed than any off the Rabbis whether they were in the Pharisaic grouping or in the grouping which maintained that the true *Halakha* was Scripture-centric and ONLY Scripture centric.
Accordingly, as we have seen, not from the beginning at Yavne -- but soon after -- this great halakhist (Rabbi El'azar) signed on to this true "New Beginning."

With the death of Rabbi Nekhunya there were now three figures who were "holding the fort" at Yavne. What fort? The fort of Scripture-centricity -- and only Scripture-centricity -- in the determining of the true Halakha.

*. ((Reprsing:
Doubtlessly Rabbi Nekhunya should not be counted here. By the time of fissure ((circa 92/94ce)) he had not been a player at Yavne having died in the very early years of the foundation of the Yavne Community. He was around during the early years of the Yavne Community but was not one who, physically, could participate in the strife-laden upheavals which came to be Yavne. He helped those who wanted to acquire what would be referred to as the "HA KATUV" orientation the heading of which pointed to "Scripture-Centricity" for both the reading of narrative sections of Scripture and also the gathering-together of the Scriptural *mitsvot* along with the analyzing, accordingly, the implications for the determining of the *Halakha* quite free of the Pharisaic orientation. Even so, without

Nekhunya insightful guidance in the early years (say in the run-up to the time of the destruction of the Temple especially but also in the opening years of the Yavne Community) it is likely that there would not even have been a Yavne/"New-Beginning" at all.

With the destruction of the Temple there was no function for the Priesthood. Nekhunya (one of the greatest OF scholars ever) in his very last years took on a moniker appropriate to a Post-Temple reality: "Rabbi Nekhunya ben Qana."))

**. {{Rabban was a shaker and a maker. Without Rabban there would never have been a Yavne. But he felt he was too old to master the new regime. He would put his energy into "leaning" on very rich Jews who understood that if the Yavne Community failed there would be no leadership for Jews. Rabban was very successful in all of this. Elsewhere I have indicated to my readers (i.e., just me) Rabban quietly followed his Oral Torah regimen.

Rabban -- without whom there would never have been a "New Beginning" at all -- was treated dastardly by the leaders of the Pharisaic Sect (the leaders of which were Rabbis Joshua and Aqiba who both -- by the way – had been mentored by Rabbi El'azar ben Hurcanus).

Rabbi El'azar also was perceived as being a "turn-coat" by most of his fellow Pharisees (and viciously by Rabbis Aqiba and Joshua) since he, Rabbis El'azar ben Hurcanus (along with Elisha ben Abuya), joined with Rabban to put his very substantial weight behind

this "new beginning." This tension has been reviewed in other portions of this book.}}
***. ((As already mentioned, Rabbi El'azar -- who had mentored Aqiba and Joshua back in his Pharisaic days -- was viciously attacked by Aqiba and Joshua on "The Day of the Coiled Snake." A very sad story as we shall see.))
****
****
****
****
****
****

PART FOUR.

End-game

The prideful and outrageous antics perpetrated by El'azar that day and memorialized in our *Baba Metsia* passage <circa in-and-around 59b-i of *Baba Metsia*; Art-Scroll pagination> were metaphorical expositions by our final anonymous editors. Metaphorical yes; but real as well; his mercurial disposition in his old age was famous; and thereby opened himself for "pay-back" <i.e., for abandoning the Pharisaic cause> by his enemies <<Rabbis Joshua and Aqiba and by extension the whole of the Pharisaic Sect at Yavne>> to take advantage of his negative demeanor>.

In this insultive attack on Rabbi El'azar, Joshua took the lead. Most certainly Rabbi Aqiba was also a major player in this attack. But Aqiba's own long history of fixation on the figure "Yeshu"/"Son-of-Man" <from *Daniel Seven*> made it prudent that he, Aqiba himself, NOT be the point person in this effort to excommunicate El'azar. After all it would be the Yeshu-connection <<along with that *min*, "The Jerusalem Community" {{attended for

some time by El'azar himself}} led by Jacob, the half-brother of Yeshu>> which would constitute the "ammunition" by which El'azar would be excommunicated.

In any case, the arguments proffered by El'azar fall into two distinct categories with the first category having two prongs.
The magical "arguments": a). commanding Carob trees <<a metaphor for the "magical" dimensions of Yeshu in particular and to a lesser degree by Jacob>> to uproot themselves and move themselves a good distance away;
and b). Commanding the waters of the canal to flow backwards; in other words the "magical" trope which always hovered -- even now towards the end of his eighth decade -- over Rabbi El'azar. Such was unfair. It was Yeshu (and to a lesser extent Yeshu's half-brother) who dabbled in the magical arts. Doubtlessly the young El'azar admired Yeshu in his adolescent years. But El'azar had, sensibly, stayed clear of the "magical" orientation of Yeshu and his half-brother. Classical "guilt by association." But in this case the "guilt by association" lingered by about a half-century. What Joshua and Aqiba orchestrated was despicable.
*****

GREAT WAS THE CALAMITY THAT BEFELL THAT DAY

Such is true. But this phrasing does not fully gauge just how AWFUL that day was. It lingered in one way or another throughout the centuries and right up to our present time. In a very fundamental way we are all still experiencing the "calamity that befell that day."

GREAT IS THE CALAMITY THAT BEFELL THAT DAY

*****

Doubtlessly El'azar did not himself deploy these arguments <<<aka the ones which are metaphors for magical/Christian practices>>> on the day when he was sabotaged by Rabbi Joshua who kept on bringing up <by *innuendo*> his <El'azar's> history with Yeshu and then with the *min* led by Yeshu's half-brother, Jacob. Rather, these "magical" practices are deployed in the text, as metaphors for what was transpiring, by our final anonymous editors, by way of ***radical indirection*** with the hope that perceptive readers would surmise what was truly going on: NAMELY, GUILT BY ASSOCIATION. These kinds of magical practices were associated with that *min* in Jerusalem led by Jacob, the half-brother of Yeshu who himself -- and on a larger level -- had been an expert in the magical arts. "Carob trees" and "water canals flowing backwards" constituted for our text an indirect way of referring to that Yeshu-oriented "Jerusalem Community" headed by Jacob, the half-brother of Yeshu. This "community" led by Jacob was radically distasteful to the majority of Jews in Jerusalem. Yes; by this time (93/94ce when the *Putsche* was being effectuated) the "Jerusalem Community was no longer in business. But bringing it up in this context, it was a reminder to the Community at Yavne that Rabbi El'azar had been tight with Yeshu.

So again; let it sink in. **Rabbi El'azar said nothing about Carob trees and canal waters flowing backwards. Nothing of the sort on this day of the "coiled" snake.**
El'azar had long since left his fascination with Yeshu-oriented matters. It would have been suicidal for his future in the Community to bring

these things up. The reality is that these "magical" actions attributed to him on that day of the "coiled snake" were put forth **by Joshua's *innuendoes***. It was a clever way of memorializing his checkered association with Yeshu himself and the Yeshu-oriented *min* led by Jacob <the half-brother of Yeshu> in Jerusalem.

(((I hope it is clear at this point that the figure of Yeshu --- along with the emergence of a Yeshu-oriented* religion in its early stage, ---- were severely upsetting to Jews with respect to the portrayals of Yeshu in the forthcoming Christian religion. The whole thing was ludicrous from beginning to end. The Gospels virtually got "gushy" in their portrayals of Yeshu. It was ridiculous. There was a wide chasm between Yeshu as he was as a Jew compared to the figure sculpted in the Gospels <albeit the Fourth Gospel is unique as we have seen>. In the Gospels -- especially in the Synoptics -- the endemic Jewishness of Yeshu is largely lost.

You might say that Yeshu was lucky in the sense that -- had he been alive <<< ----but then Yeshu would not have been the Yeshu who was on the mind of the Jews who were outraged about the way this new religion was creating fantasies at the expense of Jews ----- >>> **Yeshu himself** would be enraged by how he was being presented in the circles which would become the Christian religion. In this vein, the bottom line is one which I have deployed already:

Yeshu was born as a Jew; lived as a Jew; and died as a Jew.

In no way whatsoever would he present himself -- or have presented himself -- in any way except as being a Jew and proud thereof. He most certainly would NOT be interested in a putative religion other than

the one which owned him. He was not the founder of a "new relgion."
Yeshu was born as a Jew; lived as a Jew; and died as a Jew.

PERIOD.*

*.) A corollary of all this is *quite* revealing. When it's all said and done much of the Synoptic Gospels have created something like a "wish-fulfillment" which is impossible. A "Yeshu" straddled in his true Jewishness (((---yes there were many factions in Israel which grappled with each other; such is quintessentially Jewish, especially when it was an halakhic matter---))) with a "proto Yeshu" who wants to become what he can never become *even if he were to wish such*. But that is exactly what the Synoptics are trying to do: "squaring the circle."
As for the Fourth Gospel the *ur*-text is completely at home with Yeshu as Jewish. But that *ur*-text has been vitiated by:
a). The lateness of its appearance compared with the appearances of the Synoptics which had already vectored a version of Yeshu who is, in a manner of speaking, "Jewish-lite" at best. Thus the Fourth Gospel, even back then, is subjected to an unconscious version of "Yeshu-lite" relative to Judaism as *per* the earlier Synoptics. This means that most readers then and now bring to their accounting of Yeshu a presumption (largely unconscious of such) of "Yeshu-lite" relative to Judaism.
b). The "Hellenizing" factor which animated so much of the Fourth Gospel. This "Hellenizing" factor is virtually foreign to Yeshu's whole life.

c). The influence of Saul/Paul letters. This Saul/Paul -- who never met Yeshu at all -- had created an idiosyncratic theology which is largely out of synch with the reality of Jewish life and beliefs. Saul/Paul weaved a "Yeshu" in the image and likeness of Saul/Paul; an image which carried a gross Anti-Semitism.

d). The Hellenic background of SO many of the "Fathers of the Church." And, sadly, most of the Fathers of the Church were nurtured by the "Letters" of Saul/Paul. This "nurturing" brought with it a mean-spirited Anti-Semitism.

In other words the perception of Yeshu has been subjected to prisms ----- for almost two millennia ---- which are Foreign to the real life of Yeshu.

***** ***** *****

Continuing on:

The whole point being to the effect <recall that all of this transpired circa 93/94> that the rise of early Christianity was looked upon askance insofar as this emerging religion tended to portray a Yeshu who was *de facto* NOT the Jewish-centric reality. And the dissemination of those Letters by Saul/ Paul -- rife with the seeds of Anti-Semitism -- only made matters worse.

Jewish perception was, largely, flabbergasted that Yeshu -- who was born Jewish; who lived as a Jew; and died as a Jew – was being portrayed by the Gentiles as a figure who was, so to speak, *"Jewish Lite"*; and then, *"Jewish Lite"*-becoming something worse: **PAULINE along with its gross Anti-Semitism.**.

Enough!
****
****
****
****
****

Continuing on:
Yes indeed, it would have been suicidal (so to speak) for El'azar to have actually acted the way as he was orchestrated by our final anonymous editors. They were simply portraying -- by indirection, to be sure -- to SAY (without saying it straight out). However, the undercurrent of this famous session WAS INDEED El'azar's connection with Yeshu, primarily, and Jacob <the half-brother of Yeshu> after Yeshu died; but with a most salient distinction:
El'azar had long since put that adolescent period of his life in the past. <<And even "in the past" El'azar did not follow Yeshu (or, for that matter Jacob) in the magical practices. But the "past" didn't stay the past; rather, it was excavated from "the past" (from circa 30ce up through the present time, i.e., 93/94ce at Yavne)>>.

***** ***** ***** ***** *****
***** ***** *****
***** ***** ***** ***** *****

The backdrop was that Pharisaic ambition to take control of the Yavne Community (and thereby bringing back the Oral Torah for the determining of the *Halakha*). These two leaders of the Pharisaic Sect at Yavneh, Rabbis Joshua and Aqiba, had been tight with Rabbi El'azar back in the day **before** the move to Yavne. After all, Rabbi El'azar (((who at one time was also tight with the Pharisaic Sect

and who mentored both Rabbi Joshua and Rabbi Aqiba))) mentored both Joshua and Aqiba.
But that connection was ruptured when Rabbi El'azar threw his significant weight -- soon after the coming into being of the Yavne Community -- in the service of the orientation of "Rabbi Elisha ben Abuya." Rabbi El'azar joined the faction which was orchestrating a new approach to the determining of the *Halakha* according to Scripture-centricity and ONLY Scripture-centricity. Such was brought about by the strong belief of the founders of the Yavne Community to the effect that ----- given what had just happened to the Temple and the terrible distress by the War and Jewish life in general ----- there must be "**a new beginning**" if *Beit Yisrael* was to survive. In actual practice this meant that the Oral Torah *halakhot* so treasured by the Pharisaic faction would not be allowed at the foundational time of the Yavne Community.

Two figures -- Rabban initially and then, shortly after arriving at Yavne, Rabbi El'azar cast their very substantial weight behind this "new beginning" by way of the young leader of this "new beginning." We are speaking of Nekhunya's star pupil, "Rabbi Elisha ben Abuya." What was controversial about this "new beginning" was that the treasured *halakhot* of that putative Oral Torah would NOT be introduced in the determining of the *Halakha*. Scripture-centricity -- and ONLY Scripture-centricity -- would be the norm.
This, of course, did not sit well with the leaders and members of the Pharisaic Sect of the new Yavne Community. In fact both Rabban and Rabbi El'azar had roots in the Pharisaic-oriented Oral Torah tradition. And precisely because they had that background, they were perceived as *Turncoats*.

{{Keep in mind that the Pharisaic Sect was a majority in the Yavne Community.}}

Such simmered, always, below the surface. But, roughly, after a decade and a half there was a **growing** simmering on the part of the members of the Pharisaic faction. It grew each year. Eventually the leaders of the Pharisaic faction -- Rabbis Joshua and Aqbia were most noteworthy -- were trying to stage justifications for bringing back the Oral Torah orientation. By, roughly, 91 -- 93ce, the Pharisaic faction was **ostensibly** simmering on these matters leading to overt strife in the *Beit ha Midrash*. By 93/94, the leaders of the Pharisaic faction were ready to stage a *Coup*. The major players were Rabbis Joshua and Aqiba and the young (not yet a Rabbi) Shimon bar Yokhai. It was more or less warfare in the *Beit ha Midrash*.

*****

The leaders who stayed faithful to the foundational principles of the founding of the Yavne Community were being more and more challenged. The "Troika" <Rabban; Rabbi El'azar; and Rabbi Elisha ben Abuya <before his apostasy>; were getting not only challenged but, more and more, recipients of opprobrium (fiercely, left and right) by virtue of their own commitment relative to the validity of the foundational orientation Scripture-centricity -- and only Scripture-centricity.

*****

First there was the showdown with "Rabbi Ishmael ben Elisha." Rabbi El'azar tipped off Rabbi Elisha ben Abuya <aka "Rabbi Ishmael"> that Aqiba and Joshua were ready to ambush this Head of the *Beit haMidrash* at Yavne. Abuya was returning to his function as Head of the *Beit haMidrash* now that his mourning time for the horrific and mysterious back-to-back loss of his two sons in a very short

time period had come to a close. He carried this loss quietly even though it had been a knife-stab to his whole psyche.
Abuya was an extremely perceptive person.
He already knew about the "rumbling" which was going on the Pharisaic Sect at Yavne. He knew he would be attacked <<<and, indeed such happened>>>. He, Abuya, could read their minds. After all he had gone "face-to-face" in SO many disputes with Rabbi Aqiba and came out as having the stronger adjudication (because his, Abuya's positions were the true positions.*+**
However, what he found in his jousting with Aqiba on that fateful two-pronged session <<<<<Lauterbach; *Mekhilta De 'Rabbi Ishmael'* {vol.-ii} pages 486 --- 492>>>>> was an other dimension ----- "razor sharp and "*take no prisoners*" ----- in Rabbi Aqiba's make-up. Aqiba was always fast to be sarcastic to his enemies. But in this session there was much more than that.
He, especially, was hell-bent to "win" at any cost; indeed, by ***any*** cost.

> *. {Truth was not high in the psyche of Rabbi Aqiba. WINNING, however, was his goal; always. Yes **WINNING**; indeed, that is the proper term when one speaks of Aqiba.}
> **. {{Rabbinic Officialdom -- **long after** the sad and fateful <for *Beit Yisrael*> *denouement* of what transpired <in these back-to-back sessions (486 – 492; vol. ii of the *Mekhilta*) managed to insert into the "record" <but not so much into the *Mikhilta* Itself> some completely fatuous scenes wherein "Rabbi Ishmael" and "Rabbi Aqiba" were buddy-buddy: again, **"absolutely fatuous."**
> In any case this fateful day {{"**THE DAY THE MUSIC DIED**"}} Rabbi Aqiba's viciousness

was, shamefully, "over-the-top." {{Rabbinic Officialdom always attempted to gloss over the fateful-and-dastardly realities at Yavne in its first thirty-five years.}}

****

****

In any case, the "return" of "Rabbi Elisha ben Abuya" {{subsequent to his mourning time with respect to his two sons who had died, mysteriously, one after another without much time in between}} was one wherein Aqiba was hell-bent to viciously **destroy** the figure of Rabbi Elisha ben Abuya. Rabbi Elisha realized that it just might not go well for Rabbi Elisha.
If he -- Abuya -- were to be """"""successfully"""""" over-ruled, "Rabbi Elisha" didn't want his best student (older in age by much), "Rabbi El'azar," <<<there was so much tension at this point>>> to be smeared in the process. Elisha figured that if he, Elisha, was to be deposed as Head of the *Beit haMidrash* it would be best if "Rabbi El'azar" NOT be in attendance. If he, Elisha, ended up deposed as Head of the *Beit ha Midrash*, he didn't want any of this opprobrium to visited upon El'azar since if Elisha --- the reigning (but not for long) Head of the *Beit haMidrash* --- was in fact deposed it would be best if El'azar was NOT to be present.

"Rabbi Elisha" (-- if he, Elisha, were to deposed as Head of the *Beit haMidrah* --) would have the right to appoint a successor as Head of the *Beit haMidrah* at Yavne. Even if he were in fact deposed (and he was) he, Rabbi Elisha still maintained the power to name a successor as Head of the *Beit haMidrash* at Yavne. It was clear to Abuya that, far and away, his successor should be "Rabbi El'azar ben Hurcanus."

With all of this on his mind, "Rabbi Elisha" counselled Rabbi El'azar NOT to attend what would be a vicious show-down. If so, it would be far better if El'azar would not be in attendance for the next session. In other words, Elisha did NOT want the mercurial El'azar to be smeared by the Joshua/ Aqiba axis which was hell-bent to put the Pharisaic Sect in the driver's seat. If El'azar were brought into the ugly and vindictive quagmire he would be smeared and, possibly perceived as not worthy of the position which, by rights, would, all things being equal, have the outcome that, automatically, Rabbi El'azar would become <as *per* the rules of the *Beit haMidrash*> the Head of the *Beit haMidrash* at Yavne.

And indeed "the Record" has a certain Abba Hanin, speaking in the name of Rabbi El'azar* (which means Rabbi El'azar was NOT in in attendance), with an offering which was weak, but one which would not bring up the hackles of the Pharasaic members. All in all, Rabbi Elisha understood it would be best if in fact he (Elisha) was going to exercise his right of who would succeed him as Head of the *Beit haMidrash*; and such did come to be. It was still possible that El'azar would wound himself with some other tirade. But at least for the immediate matter Rabbi El'azar would be kept clear of any self-inflicted wound.

*. {Lauterbach; *Mekhilta De-"Rabbi Ishmael"*; volume two; pages 482-- 486.}

****
****

This time period in Elisha's life was, literally, **AWFUL.**

The wrenching and heart-breaking pain of the death of his two sons in a relatively small space of time had grievously wounded Elisha. He didn't know JUST how heart-breaking it was only when he turned back, after his period of mourning, to his position of Head of the *Beit ha Midrash* at Yavne. Those two horrendous sessions that day set in motion the vague beginning of his apostasy. Rabbi Elisha did not immediately leave the Community. While he was no longer the Head of the *Beit haMidrash*, he still attended some of the sessions. Rarely -- but not entirely -- he even offered some positions, here and there, on what was the issue of the day. But it was clear that the "Oral Torah" was taking over the very meaning of the *Halakha*. That being the case, there was no real function for him in the Community. The one still standing -- Rabbi El'azar -- was soon to be quashed by the giddy-with-power Pharisaic Sect. He would be, and was, ex-communicated.

If things really got as bad as it might, Rabbi El'azar would eventually have to stand alone when it was time for him to offer to the Community his cleverly crafted oven. But let that stand for now.
****
****

{{Find the accurate citation for me, please.}}
Aqiba : the biting of a horse and a dog etc.
It was something like this: the biting by a horse or a donkey could break bones whereas the biting by a dog does not break bones. Aqiba always went for the donkey/horse.}}
****
****

That duo [Aqiba and Joshua] was hell-bent to saddle El'azar with the *onus* of Yeshu and of his half-brother, Jacob. The "oven" was very secondary that day; a kind of fugue which, in the reality created by Joshua and Aqiba, was just a prop in the service of getting the last figure standing -- El'azar -- out of the way in the service of the Pharisaic *Putsch* which would put the final obstacle to a Pharisaic "victory"* <<<By this time Rabban had been purged; Elisha ben Abuya was drummed into apostasy; now it was the turn of El'azar>>>.
The "oven" meant nothing to these two <Joshua and Aqiba>. Just a prop for the *Putsche*.
*****
These three --- Elisha ben Abuya; Rabban; and Rabbi El'azar --- had constituted a "Troika," so to speak, who jointly (but especially Elisha ben Abuya) had followed faithfully the guiding principle of the Yavne Community: Scripture-centricity in general and Scripture-centricity with regard to determining the *Halakha*.
The Pharisaic Sect (which was a majority) felt cheated by the caveats of the ruling "Troika" <<<<<<think of Elisha ben Abuya; Rabban; and Rabbi El'azar>>>>> As for the leaders of the Pharisaic faction at Yavne Joshua and Aqiba were front and center along with the young Shimon bar Yokhai.
*****
To be sure, the fact that back in the day Aqiba -- who never met Yeshu in the flesh – maintained, for a fair amount of years, a kind of obsession with the figure of Yeshu which made it prudent that he, Rabbi Aqiba, NOT be the front-man in this attempt at a power-grab in a session wherein Rabbi El'azar would be castigated for his association with Yeshu *more than a half-century ago!*

It is not clear whether or not Aqiba truly came to eschew the figure of Yeshu on the advice of his Pharisaic colleagues. His childish fascination with the figure of Yeshu was, indeed, puerile. In any case both Aqiba and Joshua at this stage were hell-bent to have the Pharisaic faction control the Yavne Community. It was agreed, however that on this particular matter (given Aqiba's fascination with Yeshu) Rabbi Aqiba should stay in the background and let Joshua function as the lead for the embarrassing AND EXCOMMUNICATING of the "last man standing" [El'azar] of the "TROIKA" which had kept the community organization the way it founded: Scripture-centric and ONLY Scripture-centric.

*****

This "magical" Yeshu/Jacob trope was -- unfairly – glued onto El'azar. There was more than a half-century which separated the now aged Rabbi El'azar and the "still wet-behind-his-years" El'azar who, for better or for worse, admired Yeshu and who brought Yeshu to the rich homestead in Bethany. Excepting Martha -- the members of the family (and Miriam especially) of El'azar were (foolishly as it would turn out) treating Yeshu as royalty, especially by the young wet-behind-his-ears El'azar, here, and the beautiful Miriam, there.

That was yesterday and yesterday's gone

El'azar -- roughly for more than a half-century posterior to his time with Yeshu -- was, unfairly, saddled with all the negative dimensions of Yeshu and his half-brother, Jacob.

****
****
****

The point is this: that whole nexus of Yeshu and Yeshu's half-brother, Jacob, (and their correlative

activities) remained a sore spot for virtually all the participants of the Yavne Community.
Joshua, as the front man <of that Joshua/Aqiba duo>, kept banging away with these Yeshu-oriented practices and associations.

Through such indirection, our final anonymous editors were reminding readers that the days of El'azar's youth had been severely discredited by the majority faction at the Yavne Community even though he had long-since disassociated himself from those antics in the past. In any case, it was always a cloud hovering over El'azar; an onus which he carried with him even though he had genuinely "divorced" himself from those days of Yeshu and Jacob. *A fortiori*, this late in his Rabbinic career (it was in the early nineties ce) El'azar had come to have nothing but scorn for the emergence of that blossoming religion set in motion by that nut-case from Tartsus. Even so -- and regrettably so -- his early associations with Yeshu and Jacob were well known. It was El'azar's rather scandalous past of his youth and it still haunted him almost a half-century after Yeshu died.
Rabbis Joshua and Aqiba knew of El'azar's somewhat checkered past ((but blown way out of proportion in this thuggish assault on a good man)) and decided to play it up on that "day." It was they [Joshua and Aqiba and NOT El'azar] who brought up that checkered past from El'azar's very scandalous past of his youth.
In effect, Rabbi El'azar was forced to be saddled with those scandalous associations of his youth **now that he was towards the end of his eighth decade!!!!!** The most prominent association of his youth was his truly scandalous role -- played out a week before the "Great Shabbat" of that year <when Shabbat and Paseach were to be celebrated

on the same day> -- in the fake "Resurrection" orchestrated by Yeshu and the young El'azar <in a plan which had the approbation of both Caiaphas the High Priest and Pilate>. Less dramatic but almost as damning was El'azar's participation in the Jerusalem min ((led by Yeshu's half-brother Jacob)) and its celebration of the memory of Yeshu.
*****
That Yeshu-oriented min in Jerusalem was discredited by the vast amount of Jews and pre-Yavne Rabbis both while it existed <i.e., up unto the early sixties> and along-with the continuing problem constituted by some Jews who still glorified Yeshu. Certainly at Yavne all positive and open allusions to Yeshu were thoroughly discredited*. And there was no-one more adamant on this matter than "Rabbi Ishmael."

> *. {{In this regard it is VERY interesting that Rabbi Aqiba had not doused his admiration for Yeshu even after the launching of the Yavne Community. His Pharisaic colleagues made it clear to Aqiba that there would be no room for the adulation of Yeshu in this Yavne Community. ALL factions at Yavne were committed to silence <and/ or referencing the time of Yeshu and his half-brother by lavish indirection>. Indeed, the text we are reviewing here* is a good example of referring to something without saying that something in so many words. In any case, Rabbi Aqiba got the message. To be sure Aqiba maintained a positive fascination with the figure of Yeshu (although he never met Yeshu in the flesh); but he repressed this lively fascination in public lest his standing at Yavne would be compromised.

*. {{{Confer the Gemara on Tractate *Hagigah* as per page 14a-ii in the Art-Sroll rendition.}}}

*****

But the following has to be acknowledged as well. El'azar -- in his older years -- had an off-putting character defect when challenged. Under those conditions his pride, in concert with his late-in-life mercurial disposition, gave rise in El'azar's spirit to go on "the attack." This character defect made for enemies who, otherwise, might have been his allies. Joshua and Aqiba were well aware of this. Joshua was the front-man in this plan to radically demean, publically, this otherwise great Halakhist. Joshua cleverly goaded El'azar by bringing up -- by indirection (but fairly obvious indirection) -- those previous associations <<which were now serious negative baggage>> knowing full-well that doing such would send El'azar into a frenzy of polemic mercuriality so vicious that -- despite the clear and precise argumentation which supported El'azar's position -- the Community voted to excommunicate this great Halakhist. By a majority vote he was ex-communicated. <<In this vein, the reader should visit page 14a-ii of the Gemara on Tractate *Hagiga* wherein a Pharisaic colleage, Haglili, had warned Aqiba that things would not go well with him if he maintained his fascination on Yeshu.>>

****

We now turn to "c." **The Slanting Walls: *the backdrop***

At first blush one might be tempted to maintain that this portion of El'azar's presentation is simply a further metaphorical continuation of the "magic" prong of this clever setting by our final anonymous editors <i.e., the Carob trees and the backward

flow of the water in the canals>. But as we shall see, these "slanting walls" are not simply a continuation of the "magic" orientation which was foisted upon Rabbi El'azar in the service of demeaning the character of El'azar. On the contrary this segment, set in motion by "The Slanting Walls" segment of the Gemara's presentation, is far weightier than the resonations of El'azar's behavior 'back in the day' long before the founding of the Yavne Community.

This prong dealing with the 'slanting' of the walls of the *Beit haMidrash* had *immediate and present weight* quite apart from the ghosts <so to speak> back around the time of Yeshu's Crucifixion and the outrageous correlative activities at Bethany which (in an amazing turnaround) ended with Yeshu's orchestration of having the scandal be centered on himself rather than being centered on the young El'azar. This has been reviewed above.

So let us leave the ghosts of the past and deal with this major fissure in the Yavne Community (circa 93-ish).

But there is one more thing here before we grapple with the puzzling-***but weighty*** matter of the "slanting walls."

The founding of the Yavne Community had been largely orchestrated by Rabban. Rabban was the Head of the flagship *Beit haMidrash* in Jerusalem. With the onslaught of the War, it was clear that the Temple would be destroyed, and correlatively, all major vestiges of Judaism in Jerusalem including Tsakkai's flagship *Beit haMidrash*. Rabban knew that it would be a long time before Jewish Affairs in Jerusalem would safe.

Rabban (in concert with other Jews who were very, very rich) became persuaded that there would have to be for the "Chosen People" a "NEW BEGINNING." It would be some time (((and indeed this "some time," as it would turn out, the whole thing would <<<AND IS>>> drag-on for almost two millennia <albeit such would have surprised -- and more to the point --- would have deeply saddened Rabban>))) before the Jewish People could, as a People, live again in relative peace in Jerusalem.

*****

Yes: A New Beginning. The Pharisaically-oriented flagship *Beit haMidrash* in Jerusalem would no longer be the center of Jewish learning. This New Beginning at Yavne was substantially far away in the direction of EAST and slightly north of Jerusalem. Geographically that would be the "New Beginning": A Place.

Judaism really has had several "new beginnings" in its history. This one is crucial. Its indirect message ((---indirect since the final anonymous editors could not present this matter straight-on due to 'Rabbinic Offialdom"---)) was one which is an open sore <which will only get worse unless **shuvu** is executed by the majority of Jews living today> and one which couldn't, at the time of the final anonymous editors, be straight forward under the pain of never getting the precious point <"out there" in print> ***even indirectly***.

*****

Tough times sometimes birth tough solutions. This was what happened ***INITIALLY*** as the Yavne Community **became** the Yavne Community <<only to find out that the great "new beginning" came to be stifled and suffocated by the Pharisaic Sect roughly twenty years later>>.

The key to this launching <circa 70ce*> was the willingness of Rabban to throw his considerable weight on the side of those who were orchestrating this "new beginning." And not without deep paradox <<Rabban who was famous for his *Beit*

haMidrash in Jerusalem wherein the Oral Torah more or less reigned supreme>>. Rabban played the critical role in this "new beginning" for *Beit Yisrael* predicated on Scripture-centricity and ONLY Scripture-centricity for both the determining of the *Halakha* and for determining the "plain sense" for the narrative sections of the *TaNaH*.
But keep this in mind as well: although quietly he himself, without fanfare, maintained a regimen, for himself, of honoring the Oral Torah *halakhot*>.
Rabban was a "died-in-the-wool" Pharisee. And of all the Sectarian groups, the Pharasaic orientation was the largest and, arguably, the most influential.
And now we come to the paradox.
There was a Priest in the Temple who, for a number of years, gathered together scholars with an old-***but-now-new*** orientation. The Heading involved goes back **prior** to the Deuteronomic Guild. It was revised by a Temple Priest in the first century ce. His major role was Scripture Studies. After the destruction of the Temple he took on the nomenclature: Rabbi Nehunya ben Qana.
During his time in Temple duties this learn'ed Priest revived an ancient Heading and Program referred to as the HA-KATUV orientation for the study of Scripture. When the Pharisaic Sect emerged early in the Hasmonean period they "invented" <<of course that is not how they would present it>> the Oral Torah. The HA-KATUV orientation programmatically eschewed the Oral Torah invention of the Pharisaic Sect.
This "HA-KATUV" orientation had two prongs: Firstly and foremost a reading which was true to the "plain-sense" of Scripture. And secondly a set of norms by which the *mitsvot* of Scripture can be understood and deployed. It was understood in this context that the "Oral Torah" orientation of the Pharisaic Sect romance with the putative

"Oral Torah" *would not at all be integrated into this Scripture-centric --- and ONLY Scripture centric --- new beginning*.

> *. {Yes. 70ce was the founding of the Yavne Community. But the horrible displacement of a huge amount Jews because of the War with Rome and the destruction of the Temple there was "refugee" matters which occupied most of the Rabbis in those early years. By 74/75 the work of the *Beit ha Midrash* then became the center of Rabbinic matters at Yavne.}

*****

In the last five years of the Second Temple this savvy Priest tutored a small group of young students in that *old-but-now-revived* discipline referred to as this HA-KATUV orientation. One of his five students was named "Elisha ben Abuya" <<and by virtue of SAD AND MALICIOUS developments orchestrated by the leaders of the Pharisaic Sect who made it their business to resist this "New Beginning" this young "star" of this "New Beginning">> he ended up carrying the nomenclature, "Rabbi Ishmael," by which his immense offering in the first two decades of the Yavne Community his Torah studies could be woven into "The Record." His story is dispersed all throughout this presentation.

This prodigy was relatively young. But his prodigious knowledge of Scripture in general and of the ins and outs of the *mitsvot* of Scripture set this young genius apart from all the others. Tsakkai at this time was investigating the set of scholars and Rabbis which would follow him to the "New Beginning" at Yanve. Tsakkai was fascinated with both Nehunya the Priest and his star pupil, Elisha ben Abuya.

Rabban was, so to speak, a card-carrying member of the Pharasaic Sect. However, the very NATION of *Yisrael* was now in dire straits. Rabban was very much affected -- especially in this time of incredible upheaval for *Erets Yisrael* -- by the slogan: *If nothing changes, nothing changes.* Tsakkai knew in his heart that he would honor -- more or less secretly -- the Oral Torah *halakhot* as well as the *mitsvot* of Scripture as HIS PERSONAL commitment and, further, and with having no notion that others would follow in this private decision.

That having been stipulated, Rabban understood that *Beit Yisrael* was in dire straits (((indeed it might have been totally blown away))). Innovation ----- yes extreme innovation ---- was required for there be a chance for *Beit Yisrael* to survive. Accordingly he put his majorly hefty and respected weight behind this "New Beginning" <<<<which programmatically DID NOT recognize the Pharisaic-Sect's Oral Torah orientation given that the determining of the *Halakha* was to be determined according to Scripture-centricity and ONLY Scripture-centricity.>>>>

Yes. He would end up as being seen as a "Turncoat" to his fellow Pharisees and he was subjected to a heartbroken ending orchestrated by those two major leaders of that Pharisaic faction at Yavne <Rabbis Joshua and Aqiba>. But this "New Beginning" at Yavne required a kind of filtering out of the status of that ever-proliferating invention of the Oral Torah *halakhot*.

All that is true and Rabban -- the Head of this new *Beit haMidrash* – did not rescind at all the new regimen. But -- let us note yet again -- in his heart he would still, quietly, maintain for his **private** life, the *halakhot* of the Oral Torah (and, of course the *mitsvot*).

Yes. This too. As it turned out, Rabban was metaphorically "crucified" <so to speak> for this innovation. He paid a huge price. But Tsakkai did the right thing.

*****

All of the above was necessary to set the stage of the outcome of "***the slanting walls***." In fact the "slanting walls" are still slanting, except NOW there is little hope that the "slanting walls" can be rectified. Indeed, we are closer than ever to time when the walls will totally collapse. Such would mean -- if we really understand the precarious metaphor -- the end of *Beit Yisrael*. It is that serious.

****

****

****

Baba Metsia 59a-iii ----- 59b-iii.

The Slanting Walls 59b-i.

There are several huge matters which were imbued into our text. Staccatically:

One valid way of looking at these texts is the matter of "majority rules." One might maintain that some of the greatest harms throughout history in general -- and also in the history of Judaism -- are a function of "majority rules." That is why there is a saying:

the tyranny of the majority

As an opener I suggest that what happened on this day of the "coiled snake" is a good case in point of the danger -- the very real and deep danger -- of "*majority rules.*"

As we have seen in this section of the relevant Gemara <*Baba Metsia* in and about 59a-iii ---- 59b-ii of the Art-Scroll rendition> Joshua is deploying ----- <in the context of a heated back

and forth between Rabbi El'azar and Rabbi Joshua> ----- a short snippet from *Exodus* 23:2 ***thereby suppressing the context wherein the snippet is located***. {{{{I must repeat that; the whole meaning of this section is the above:

----- a short snippet from *Exodus* 23:2 ***thereby suppressing the context wherein the snippet is located***.}}}}

Let it sink in.
And as well the fatuous way Joshua* ((((but it was Aqiba who culled Scripture to find SOME 'fig-leaf' phrase lifted out of the whole "plain sense" of *Exodus* 23:2 from the verse in question)))) treats Scripture. To wit:

Herewith the snippet ***lifted by -- out of its context*** -- from *Exodus* 23:2:

According to the majority the matter shall be decided.

This is terrifically problematic; let me count the ways:
i). The Hebrew word in question is **n'eebbar** <from right to left>. The word has a plethora of meanings and is cognate with other Hebrew cousins of it. In the translations I have checked out the word "<the> multitude" seems to be the chosen translation along with "<the> mighty>."
Yes, in the context from our *Baba Metsia* Gemara the word "<the> majority" would be acceptable in certain contexts, albeit though, our text from Exodus 23:2 **does not** offer any semantic indication ***at all*** that the "n'eebbar" in this verse the word "majority" should be deployed in its present context of Exodus 23:2. **Indeed quite to the contrary:** "majority" does not catch the context of n'eebbar **when one is speaking in the context of Exodus 23:2.** Indeed Joshua's deployment of the verse **VIOLATES** the "plain-sense" of *Exodus* 23:2.

ii). Keep in mind that the spirit of the germane text <<Exodus 23:2 along with its continuation through verse three>> ***is totally focused on the "moral/ ethical" plane***.

iii). In contrast, "Majority Rules" is not so much a moral/ethical matter as it is a pragmatic matter. With that understanding it turns out that the to-be-the-case deployment of "majority <rules>" the "n'eebbar" in question ---- (and this is the ugly spirit of what was going on with Rabbi Joshua's outburst **out of context**) --- is making its Scriptural justification on the plane of "majority rules" {which comes from Humans; not from God} **even when it is clear that in the case of 23:2 the matter is on the Moral/ethical Plane.** In effect, Joshua's claim bypasses the "plain-sense" of Scripture in favor of a manipulation of words to justify what Rabbis Joshua and Aqiba are planning to do: A PUTSCH TO GAIN POWER IN THE YAVNE COMMUNITY.*

> *. {In other words Joshua's outburst clearly deploys the **m'eebbar** <from right to left> as "majority." So-be-it. Accordingly, then, there are valid deployments of **m'eebbar** with the connotation of "majority." "Majority Rules" may or may not has its place and time in other situations **HOWEVER**, in the context of *Exodus* 23:2 the meaning for **m'eebbar** as "majority" **is jarringly out of place.** Any fair reading of *Exodus* 23:2 would reveal that a moral matter is at work. Hashem speaking:
>
> **You shall** [neither] **not side with the multitude to do wrong** -----
> **You shall** [neither] **not side with the mighty to do wrong -----**
> **You shall** [neither] **not side with the majority to do wrong -----**

[It is the third rendition which is found in the JPS.]

Fine.

On the other hand, the phrasing of the third sentence, **could** ((all depending on context, of course)) have another flavor:

You shall [neither] **not side with the majority**<in the sense of **"majority rules" in a voting matter**>**.**

We have already noted that it is this last meaning which animates Rabbi Joshua's contention. And as we have seen "majority rules" may be a pragmatic solution in many situations; on the other hand the principle of "majority rules" is, often enough, a principle for horror. Have we forgotten that Hitler came to power by "Majority Rules"?

*****

Yes, of course. I have read the footnote of Art Scroll [*Baba Metsia*; 59b-I; footnote #6; Art-Scroll pagination] which makes an attempt to defend the putative need of allowing a "majority rules" caveat in some situations. But **this** situation does not justify such a compromise. Leave it as an open question whether or not "majority rules" does more damage or less damage. In any case my claim has little to do with such prognosticators for and against "majority rules."

There is a far more valuable issue put on the table by Joshua's putative <and bad faith> citation of *Exodus* 23:2.

Any fair reading of 23:2 would disclose that the spirit of Joshua's fuzzy outburst **actually goes against the clear spirit of Exodus 23:2.** Indeed the moral/ethical matter of 23:2 ***doesn't even intersect with EITHER opinion on "Majority Rules***." To use 23:2 as a defense for Joshua's **is despicable**.

There is no doubt that Joshua (but it was really Aqiba who is "good" at ***finding*** these strange readings of Scripture) deployed the word **m'eebbar** <right to left> in bad faith insofar 23:2, read in its context, clearly does NOT substantiate a "majority rules" reading of this verse which obtains solely on the moral/ethical plane. Shame on Joshua; Shame on Aqiba.
*****

For the Record:
Exodus 23:2
Joshua was the point man while, in this episode, Aqiba -- contrary to his disposition to be the "star" -- did the Scriptural work behind the scene. Finding this verse (with its nuances which allow for more than one interpretation of the verse) was the work of Aqiba and executed by Joshua. It worked. "It worked" at the expense of skull-drudgery. Shame on Joshua; Shame on Aqiba.}
****
****
****
****
****

Yes. In this review of that calamitous day I thought it better to delineate the outcome as an introduction to the real underlying matter which is revealed by the "Slanting Walls" of the *Beit ha Midrash*. The "Slanting Walls" episode is one which was never truly adjudicated. It is an age-old story wherein Truth --- the very Seal of Hashem --- quietly undermines, in the long run, the misuse of Power by those who should know better. Then

again, in the short run, Power prevails; such is a sad dimension of *Beit Yisrael*. If it should ever come to be the case that the prevailing misuse of majority Power throttles the Seal of Hashem decisively then all is lost. But truth has it wiles and ways as well. The Slanting Walls remain with us today. Let us now jump over the metaphors and engage directly the truth of things in these Jewish matters.
Our friend El'azar was and is the key. What goes on in a true *Beit ha-Midrash* is our only hope. Yes; bitter tension trumps a final disaster.* This is an old story. It is draped with "good intentions" which, somehow, always fall short. Time, so it seems, is no longer to be presumed to continue forever; there is, after-all, an end of time.

> *. [Yes. Then again, in the long run, Power tends to prevail. Such has been, within *Beit Yisrael*, the sad dimension of *Beit Yisrael* AND IT CONTINUES IN OUR TIME. Time after time **SHUVU!** Is ignored -- or worse -- given lip service without changing. *If nothing changes **nothing changes***. The continued existence of *Beit Yisrael* has come to a final turning point.
> Most of all, listen from the *Devarim* redactor.

Davarim 30:11--14. To wit:

For this mitsva *I am laying down for you today is neither obscure for you nor beyond your reach. It is not in the heavens so that you need to wonder:* "Who will go up the heavens and bring it down for us." *Nor is it beyond the seas such that you would say:* "Who will cross the seas to get it for us and tell us of it."

NO:

It is something near to you: in your mouth and in your heart to put it in practice.

]

****
****
****
****
****

Continuing on.
Let us cut to the chase. This whole portion is critical. Carob trees uprooting themselves transporting themselves far away; water flowing backward. All of this is, in a manner of speaking, just an introduction. It is a clever way by our final anonymous editors to put forth to their readers that the backdrop of this whole session -- drummed up by Joshua and Aqiba -- is a reminder to the voters in the *Beit haMidrash* that Rabbi El'azar was very close those two "magicians" -- Yeshu and his half-brother Jacob -- who without actually trying to start a new religion nevertheless constituted the fodder for that deeply flawed man from Tartsus who pretty much was the midwife of Christianity.*

*. [Yes. It is true that Jacob saw through the man who arrived at his *min* several years after Yeshu died. This "Saul/Paul" fellow lusted to be famous. While he did -- albeit as a *mamzer* -- come from a Jewish family this fellow had never been trained in Jewish Law. Jacob's *min* was totally committed to the dietary *mitsvot*. Saul/Paul thought that such was stupid. There were clashes between the two. Jacob settled on getting him out of the *min* by offering to Saul/Paul the mandate of "Apostle to the Gentiles." It was a huge mistake. This Saul/Paul figure took it seriously. In the process he wrote those "Letters." There was very little in those Letters which was really Jewish.

> Further, in those Letters he invented a "Yeshu" who clearly was not Jewish. As for the *Halakha* Saul/Paul would have nothing to with it. Finally, if you are excavating the seeds of Anti-Semitism you do not have to search much further than those "Letters." Jacob made a HUGE mistake with his suggestion that this excuse of a man should become the "Apostle to the Gentiles." Jacob should have thrown this excuse of a human from the *min* on the second day of his sojourn.]

So let us put to bed the tributaries which became the rivers of Christianity. We turn back to Rabbi El'azar -- now a mercurial old man -- who was, in effect, the central character of the Yavne drama.

*****

Again: The matter of the "Slanting Walls."

Usually I stay pretty close to the "plain-sense" of the text itself. But what was going to be -- and it was already partly on its destined way -- the treatment herewith to come cuts through the metaphors. The metaphors, in the final analysis, are not sufficient. The metaphors must cut to the truth. And without the truth there will be no life; at all.

The *Beit ha Midrash* at Yavne was orchestrated by a few visionaries who had seen beyond the oncoming destruction of the Temple. *Beit Yisrael* had failed in its mission; so far.

The leading lights were Rabban; Rabbi Nekhunya ben Qana (who had been a Temple Priest); the young-but-gifted <exceptionally gifted> Rabbi Elisha ben Abuya who had been mentored by Rabbi Nekhunya; and -- not right away but relatively soon after the foundation of the Yavne -- Rabbi

El'azar became one of the leading lights in the Community.
The Head of the *Beit ha Midrash* at Yavne was <until he apostatized> Rabbi Elisha ben Abuya. Rabban was the Head of the whole Community. He was not so gifted in the new HA KATUV orientation, especially since his strongest suit was the "Oral Torah" orientation of the Pharisaic Sect. And one knows, by this time, that the *Beit haMidrash* at Yavne was married to "Scripture-centricity" -- and ONLY Scripture-centricity -- in all matters and especially with regard to determining the *Halakha*. Rabban seldomly led any sessions at the *Beit ha Midrash*. His higher calling was to raise the money to keep the Community intact.
Then there was the case of El'azar ben Hurcanus. He didn't get tight with the founders from the very beginning. But as El'azar came into often contact with Rabbi Elisha ben Abuya he came to have a high admiration for Rabbi Elisha ben Abuya and Abuya's "Gospel" of Scripture-centricity and ONLY Scripture-centricity.

> *. {There would never have been a "new beginning" for the Rabbinic Movement without the tremendous money and energy which Tsakkai brought to this "new beginning. He would eventually be sandbagged by Rabbis Aqiba and Joshua (stalwart Pharisees) and forced out of the Community at the beginning of the *Putsche* starting in 93ce and into 94ce. The Pharisaic faction at Yavne was NOT AT ALL happy with the constraint that the *Halakha* would have to be determined by Scripture-centricity and ONLY Scripture-centricity. Sandbagging Rabban -- orchestrated by Rabbis Joshua and Aqiba -- was a disgrace. Rabbis Aqiba and Joshua would never

have had ANY substantial Rabbinic career without this giant figure.}

****

****

****

****

****

The Slanting Walls. {59b-i --- 59b-ii}
Permit, if you will, if I cut to the chase and leave behind the metaphoric presentation.
The tension at Yavne has everything to do with the status of the Oral Torah claim SO dear to those who were weaned on their on their Mother's milk: The Oral Torah.
On the other hand there was the "New Beginning" championed by Rabbi Elisha ben Abuya and backed by the powerful backing of Rabbi Yochanan ben Tsakkai. It would not be long before Rabbi El'azar ben Hurcanus joined in what might be called a Troika. "Majority Rules" was quite definitely NOT the guiding principle of the "New Beginning." Rather, the guiding principle was Scriptural-centricity with respect to maintaining the "plain-sense" of the Scripture narratives along with Scripture-centricity in the determining of the *Halakha*.
It was Elisha ben Abuya who offered to the leaders of the Pharasaic Sect that the treasured Oral Torah *halakhot* could be maintained as *minhaggim*. This offer was not accepted as sufficient by the leaders of the Pharasaic Sect.

*****

The Troika ((and I use that term not sarcastically but simply as a heading of who was in charge)) ran the *Beit haMidrash*
Long story short:

The members of the Pharisaic Sect were a majority faction. They groused over the limitations imposed on them.
*****
This went on for almost two decades. Some people such as Rabbi Aqiba looked for "loopholes" during the sessions. They were always cleanly stifled by Elisha ben Abuya. It bothered not only Rabbi Aqiba but other strong personalities in the Pharasaic Sect. Aqiba, however, never gave up trying. ((Perhaps he tried something else.))

***** ***** *****

It was a tragedy which brought about change in the Yavne Community.

Mysteriously, the two sons of Rabbi Elisha ben Abuya were found dead -- first the one and about a week later for the other one -- in their own home. This was a horrible blow to Rabbi Elisha. He would never again be the same. He was weakened in his ability to maintain the regimen of which he was in charge: i.e., leading the sessions of the Beit haMidrash.* After Elisha's mourning period Elisha returned and continued to lead the sessions. Again, it is noteworthy, that Elisha's spirit was very low. In the meantime the leaders of the Pharisaic Sect started to flex their muscles more and more following the lead of Rabbi Aqiba. The turning point was a very disruptive back-to-back of two sessions in the Beit ha Midrash dealing with the thrice-deployed text in Scripture concerning boiling a kid in its mother's milk.
Notes on these two uproarious back-to-back sessions can be found on pages 486 through 492 in Tractate "Kaspa" of volume II of the Lauterbach presentation of the **Mekhilta de 'Rabbi Ishmael.'** {{In other words when the notes on these many

sessions <<which was led by Elisha ben Abuya and which would come to comprise this "Mekhilta de 'Rabbi Ishmael' ">> were compiled long after the apostasy of Elisha ben Abuya. By that time it was forbidden to cite the teachings under the rubric "Rabbi Elisha ben Abuya" since he had apostatized. Accordingly, a cognomen -- orchestrated by Rabbi Judah much later -- was used instead of his true name. This cognomen was "Rabbi Ishmael ben Elisha" which, more often, was simply put forth as "Rabbi Ishmael." It was "Rebbe" -- long after "Akher" apostatized -- who settled on "Rabbi Ishmael ben Elisha" <usually simply "Rabbi Ishmael"> as a cognomen so that the HUGE Torah Wisdom of this Giant at Yavne could be entered into the "Record."}}}

*****

Reprising:

Sooner or later there was bound to be major repercussions. First of all were the deaths -- in fairly rapid succession -- of his sons which were taken away from him. His spirits, quite naturally were low; very low. Today we would refer to his condition as suffering in a deep depression.

When Elisha revived himself sufficiently enough to return to leading the sessions <<<Rabbi El'azar had substituted for him>>> he lacked the verve which he used to have. His Pharisaic colleagues challenged him more and more. By hook or by crook they saw an opportunity to expand the parameters of the *Beit ha Midrash*. And it was clear that it was more and more difficult for Elisha to make comebacks from their stream of challenges. The writing was on the wall. Elisha came to realize that sooner or later the Pharisaic Sect at Yavne would, eventually, take over the orientation of what was acceptable and what was not acceptable. He now fully understand that it would soon be

the case that the Pharisaic Sect would be running the *Beit ha Midrash* and ultimately in accordance largely with the Oral Torah orientation.
Yes. The leaders of the Pharisaic Sect made sure that they did not denigrate the *mitsvot* of Scripture. But it was clear to Elisha that it would only be a matter of time before -- *de facto albeit not promulgated as such* -- the Oral Torah would reign supreme in the *Beit ha Midrash*.

Elisha understood that the day would becoming -- and soon -- when there would be no more room at Yavne for a "true" *Halakha*, namely a *Halakha* rooted in Scripture-centricity and only Scripture-centricity. And as it would turn out, the *coup de grace* came rather quickly. For the next Biblical matter was that somewhat mysterious caveat <<<<each rendition of which would end up in three different deployments, each standing by itself and largely out of the surrounding tracts immediately prior and immediately posterior from the narrative which surrounding these three deployments>>>> --------- a caveat largely standing by itself and largely out of the context in which it appeared:

Thou shalt not seethe a Kid in its mother's milk {*Exodus* at 23: 19; *Exodus* at 34:26; and *Devarim* at 14:21}

*****

For almost five centuries the Pharsaic Sect had focused on this thrice articulated mandate as a dietary mandate. It was rather fetishistic the way they tried to protect the **presumed dietary** character of this ***curious*** thrice--articulated mandate. And, as we shall see just below, the Pharisaic faction was to go to almost **ANY MANNER WHATSOEVER** -- come hell or high water -- to continue their homage to the thrice-articulated mandate. All in the service of maintaining a dietary meaning for our thrice articulated mandate and thereby suffocating the sacred import of this thrice-articulated mysterious revelation which clearly points beyond its literal meaning.

By insisting on such a literal and dietary (thrice-deployed, mind you) meaning to this mandate the Pharisaic Sect achieved a hollow and spurious "victory" and, in so doing, drowning-out the sacred **HOLY WARNING** executed by an anonymous redactor who was trying to awaken *Beit Yisrael* to its highest calling.*

> *. {{{Yes, of course. There are literal readings of Scripture and then there is the "Plain Sense" of Scripture. The literal reading of Scripture is impoverished in so far as -- being only a literal reading of Scripture -- is mostly unable to carry to the reader to the context of what is being said. On the other hand, it is always wise to start with a literal reading insofar as doing such enables accuracy in achieving the "plain sense" of Scripture. Famously it is "Rabbi Ishmael ben Elisha" (aka "Rabbi Elisha ben Abuya"; aka
> "Akher") who insists on the "plain sense" of Scripture in contrast to the shenanigans of Rabbi Aqiba who often mangled the "plain-sense" by abusing what might be called the trivia of Scripture <e.g., those famous "*ets*," etc.> in the service of idiosyncratic readings which putatively bolsters some angle for support for a reading which, for example, which would bring in the Oral Torah orientation into such a reading. To wit:

All of that being said, it was Rabbi Elisha ben Abuya who understood that **WHEN SCIRPTURE ITSELF** consciously advertises an idiosyncratic promulgation ((i.e., the curious and thrice-deployed mandate:

Thou shalt not seethe a Kid in its mother's milk

)) then the "plain sense" takes a holiday. And such is rare; very rare. It is Scripture's way of pointing to something nuanced and quite important, as we shall see.
We can put it this way:

Finally there is the rare case wherein Scripture speaks idiosyncratically. This is the situation with the three (and somewhat mysterious) deployments ((largely out of context)) of that thrice-articulated caveat.}}}
****
****
****

Rabbi Elisha ben Abuya, however, had come prepared for this. It was clear that this thrice-executed caveat was totally **idiosyncratic**. To be sure, Rabbi Elisha ben Abuya, was famous for insisting on the "plain sense" of Scripture. On the other hand, when there was an a clear and jarring **idiosyncratic** character to some verse or statement of Scripture Rabbi Elisha ben Abuya reasoned that with SUCH an idiosyncratic offering <**and thrice deployed without any clear context AT ALL in all three CASESl**>, the "plain sense" of the offering had to be itself idiosyncratic and/or something of metaphorical weight. In this *Mekhilta* passage Rabbi Elisha ben Abuya settled on three nodal points from Scripture which would honor the

clearly -- AND SACRED -- idiosyncratic import of the thrice-articulated mandate.
With a stroke of genius "Rabbi Elisha" <<<much much later to be known as "Rabbi Ishmael ben Elisha> by-passed the dietary meaning ((which, as we shall see below takes something of grandeur and degrades it to something pedestrian)) in favor of something truly Holy: THE SACRED COVENANT.
Probing Scripture, Rabbi Elisha put forth three historical times and places wherein the Sacred Covenant was validated: One at Horeb <*Ex.* 24: 7-8>; one on the plains of Moab <*Devarim* 29-11>; and one at Mounts Gerizim and Mount Ebal <ibid. 28-69>.
It is most significant that Rabbi Elisha's offering totally eschews any *dietary* <direct or indirect> interpretation of the thrice articulated mandate.**In contrast (and Rabbi El'azar was one by proxy <see below>) the others who offered interpretations that were either directly dietary in nature and/or matters ancillary to a dietary interpretation of the thrice-articulated mandate. Keep that in mind.*

*. [Even Rabbi El'azar is cited as allowing a dietary dimension for this thrice-articulated <albeit by proxy> caveat.]

**. [There is also this. The first to bring up an interpretation to succeed the NON-DIETARY offered by "Rabbi Ishmael" was Rabbi Josiah, who was the star mentee of Rabbi Elisha." Rabbi Josiah <<and for that matter, Rabbi Jonathan, another gifted mentee of Rabbi Elisha>> was not a member of the Yavne Community. They were both from "the South" of *Yisrael*. When they heard of the horrible deaths of Elisha's two sons they made it their business to come to the vicinity of the Yavne

Community so as to comfort their great mentor. They stayed until Elisha was ready to take up again his position as Head of the *Beit haMidrash* at the Yavne Community. However!:
Josiah did not necessarily endorse nor eschew his mentor. Even Josiah was surprised at his mentor's offering. "Surprised" does not equate to "rejection." If you read Rabbi Josiah's offering you will quickly see that he had a nuanced accounting of the thrice-articulated mandate. It touches on a dietary interpretation, but his full accounting cannot be reduced to a simple dietary accounting. The other mentee of Rabbi Elisha was present as well: Rabbi Jonathan who offered a short accounting more or less on the plane of a dietary interpretation.]

****
****
****
****

You are now mandated to meditate on what transpires on pages 237 <i.e., from the heading "The Day The Music Died" on page 237 through the first paragraph on page 265 of the book under discussion <see below>. I will put forth here **some** segments from those pages. However, much which is contained on this matter is found only in the book you are NOT reading right now. In any case, herewith the true title of that Book:

vaT meM felA
then
!UVUHS

In this vein, much of what Rabbi Elisha put forth in the two back-to-back sessions are found on the pages of the *Mekhilta* <volume ii; pages 489 ---- 492>. A major part of these two back-to-back sessions includes how he was viciously challenged across the board by his Pharisaic enemies on these pages of the *Mekhilta*. We shall touch on some of these matters in THIS production.

There was a mix-up between the publisher and myself concerning how the title of the book-**cover** was to be presented. Accordingly, you should not use the title as it appears on the front cover. The true title is just above and it is also properly deployed on the title PAGE

ISBN: 978-1-4575-4271-8
Dog Ear Publishing
4011 Vincennes Rd
Indianapolis, IN 46268
www.dogearpublishing.net

If you try to purchase the book from the publisher there MIGHT be a problem. It is a publishing operation which, apparently, does not produce single books insofar as they make their money by way of bulk purchases. Perhaps they would make an exception. If not, contact me at 570-241-8074 and I'll provide the book (subject to the number of copies I will have had at the time).

****
****

Please add on to your reading assignment. It continues -- with drama -- what is said above concerning the thrice-articulated mandate.

The tension during these two back-to-back sessions is IMMENSE. You will be flabbergasted.

Try to get a copy of *Mikhilta de "Rabbi Ishmael."* Start from page 486 and take it through 492. There will be a surprise on each page. In particular you should read carefully pages 488 through 492. I refer to these passages as the ***NO!*** pages. Rabbi Elisha clearly was rattled by the furious verbal assaults visited upon him by Rabbi Aqiba. The whole thing was an ambush. And, in the eyes of Rabbi Aqiba, such was "successful." "Successful," that is, if raw power trumps truth. Rabbi Elisha did not return to the fray. He did stay in the Community for about a month but he did not participate in the *Beit ha Midrash*. It was over for him.

He understood that this was the first, but decisive, "win" which set on motion the deposing of Rabban and, last but not least, Rabbi El'azar. Again, he stayed around Yavne for about a month posterior to those horrific sessions.

So yes. Apostasy was the only possible outcome. When the Pharasaic Sect will have deposed both Rabban and, last but not least, Rabbi El'azar, the Pharisaic Sect will have been "victorious."

We are STILL the heirs of this un-godly *Putsch*. And the whole make-up of *Beit Yisrael* is -- largely unaware -- going through the motions. The cancer of the Oral Torah is almost complete. And when (and if????-- I still have hope) *Beit Yisrael* disappears from our planet, it will not be long after that the whole of humanity will follow.

If nothing changes, **NOTHING CHANGES**.

****
****
****
****
****
****

****
****

Continuing on:

Do you get it yet? It is NOT Akher who must **RETURN!/*SHUVU!***: the command-which-is-also-a-plea.
Akher was not being stubborn. The great tension then and now (albeit it is largely a suppressed tension) is the status of the Oral Torah (and its accoutrements) *vis a vis* Scripture-centricity for the determining of the *Halakha*. The final anonymous editors had to use subterfuge phrasing in order to even get certain ideas and norms into the *Bavli* at all.
LISTEN:
The Oral Torah comes from the Pharisees, not from God. Its weight on the *Halakha* is terribly over-bearing. Basically, for the Orthodox, the Oral Torah has become a false god.
In contrast, for the rest of the non-Orthodox Sects of Judaism it doesn't really matter. Lip service is accorded to many things Jewish by the non-Orthodox communities; but actual practice is rather thin and "surfacey." 'Pick-and-Chose.' The Synagogues which are built -- especially in the Diaspora -- are grand edifices which are finding fewer and fewer "visitors" (that word is appropriate). Sects which never probe. Much is claimed but only on the surface. In contrast over in Orthodoxy Land (whether in the Diaspora or in *Erets Yisrael*) there is constant motion and activity without true substance.
It can't go on like this. But, I suspect, it will. *If nothing changes nothing changes.*
*****

"Modern Orthodoxy." Is that a solution? It certainly will not if it does not budge from the *de facto* hegemony of the Oral Torah. Who is listening?

****
****

In this vein I would like to pause at this time and celebrate Jacob Lauterbach. Him in particular. But let the name also stand as a kind of Paradigm for all those who are engaged -- with the proper credentials and love of research -- with Jewish Scholarship.

I realize that some people might even make the case that praise from someone such as me is a disservice to the memory of Jacob Lauterbach. Or even worse think of a mouse who stumbles across a big piece of cheese. The mouse is overwhelmed by the size of the cheese. But he still nibbles away. If that's all I am, then so be it.

I am not a scholarly kind of guy by a long stretch. I am a writer. Writers write.

Think of me ((if you even deign to think of me)) as a story-teller. For some time now my heart and mind has been centered on Judaism. Judaism is not, *per se*, a pathology. **NO! Quite the opposite**. If *Beit Yisrael* should die out then soon after all of humanity will die out. The continuation of the human race is predicated on the survival of *Beit Yisrael: The People; The Land; and the Religion; in that order.* Should such a calamity as the non-survival of *Beit Yisrael* will morph into the final calamity of the human race.

All of that stipulated, there ARE pathologies in Judaism; far and away.

With regard to my interest in Judaism, some would say (and who is sure that they are not right) words to this effect:

It is virtually blasphemous (and ludicrous to boot) *that this goy-boy* [I am now seventy-one] *putative convert* (a conversion the validity of which some would challenge) *would presume to jump in ---willy-nilly*--- into some of the most sacred dimensions of Judaism. Indeed you may be inclined to order a* Beit Din *to the effect that these writings on Judaism by* "Hullin" *are "strictly anathema, now and forever."*

But Spinoza survived.

*. ["*willy-nilly*" is now the only way I can still write. But don't beg the question. **IF** truth comes by a "*willy-nilly*" merchant (let's add on that he had scabs all over his body to get the idea across) your merchant (not of Venice but New Jersey) with a back-pack of gold who was interested in *donating!* the whole kit-and-kabooble <no strings attached> you would find a way ((I certainly would find a way if our destiny roles were different)) to accept the gift.]

I understand all of the above and more. Whether or not it is my *mazzal* I don't know. Perhaps it's just an insidious layer of my soul. I don't know.

*****

But let's get back to Lauterbach. We do share in common: we are both writers. He was a writer and a scholar. I am only a writer.

Call me a story-teller. And then waken up to the fact that some stories CAN be true.

Stories can be fiction and stories can be true. And sometimes they are really stories and are true. I am hopelessly drawn to writing, for better or for worse. I hope I am not **just** writing fiction. But maybe I am.

For much more than a decade I have been writing stories about the various facets of Judaism. The roots of my fascination for and about Judaism

involves some sad moments some of which are horrifying.
****
****

Of course one knows that the highest Revelation is by way of the *CHUMASH*; and that the second highest Revelation is by way of *Nevi-im*. Good. And it is said that *Ketuvim* is bereft of Revelation; albeit much wisdom comes from it as well. That's fine. But consider this: sitting outside of a two story house <<i.e., the *Chumash* and *Nevi-im*>> on its side lawn while the windows are open. Some waft of Revelation – i.e., we are speaking of *Ketuvim* -- does come through the windows especially in Spring and Summer. There is indeed a kind of soft covering of distilled Revelation (in this case *Ketuvim*) which does come from the two-story home.
****
****
****

Continuing on.
Back to our thrice-articulated mandate.
*****
I want to make the following clear. The various ways by which the thrice-articulated mandate was -- by the Pharisaic faction -- understood in an exclusively dietary manner has led to a plethora of sub-mandates relative to mixing milk and meat. Whatever is said in this production it will nevertheless probably ((and this just by itself was a HUGE mistake in the history of *Beit Yisrael*)) be the case that this thrice-articulated mandate will -- wrongfully as we shall see below -- continue to be observed in the genus of dietary matters. And, in

fact, such is acceptable on a certain level <but not on the ***truest*** level.
Let these dietary interpretations of the thrice-articulated mandate (each instantiation being, in varying manners, out of Scripture's immediate context wherein they are found) be maintained, if wanted, as treasured *minhaggim*. On the other hand, forcing this most idiosyncratic verse in our whole of Scripture to be circumcised as a purely dietary mandate is, in fact, to misread in bad faith the radical and holy significance of this oddest part of Scripture. Doing such is a serious **violation** of Scripture. The reality is that the significance of our thrice-articulated mandate in Scripture is orders of magnitude more fundamental than the dietary <<that is, the ones which are Scripturally valid>> mandates.

And please do not understand me. Scripture's **valid** <i.e., Scripture born> dietary mandates ARE crucial for the life of Judaism.
*****
For the present time it is enough to ponder what we all know: HOW AWFUL -- and in this sentence I refer to animals only -- it would be to seethe a KID in its OWN MOTHER'S milk. The hearer (regardless of the language deployed) of such would, at the least, be squeamish by reading that phrase or hearing that phrase for most people. It conjures up something ugly on the Human plane even though the two participants are the putative mother goat and the *KID*. Yes. Again, <u>of course</u>, we are not literally talking about human mothers and their offspring. Nonetheless the **words themselves** conjure up, ***<u>of themselves</u>***, something dreadful. And that is the point.
Our canny redactor who deployed this mandate into our Sacred Scripture knows that the

phrasing being deployed conjures up -- one way or another -- something deeply blasphemous and horrendous on the Human plane. It gets our attention. ((In other words, the thrice-articulated mandate automatically conjures up some such scene wherein a human offspring is being boiled <possibly alive> in ITS OWN MOTHER'S MILK <<but does not say so in so many words>>)).
To be sure, the subtle Deuteronomist who inserted this thrice-articulated mandate knew exactly what thoughts and images would be conjured up *simply by articulating the sentence at hand. In effect, the very wording conjures up other horrific scenarios which would sicken any decent human and which would have the effect of generating in the sensitive reader "a wake-up call" with respect to the HUGE amount of atrocities which humans visit upon other humans.*
Could it be that our clever redactor is subtly "saying thoughts" to this effect?:

We all sin and we all have regrets ((sometimes HUGE regrets)) for our actions. This thrice-articulated mandate, however, -- not literally but in fact – conjures up the horror potential of each and every grown human. You and Me.
It is a **warning** *in effect. Each one of us is liable of being a monster.*

Accordingly: The true force of the thrice-articulated mandate is to the effect of being a ***warning***. Again: we all sin. If we then let ourselves become monsters then there is no turning back. The thrice- articulated mandate is a warning. {{Yes. It had to be repeated.}} A warning for all of us:

You do not HAVE to be a monstor; you can still "turn" back.* [shuvu] But if you allow your spirit to become a monstrous spirit, *you will be lost

forever. You will deny that any images come to your mind involving an offspring* {a kid} *being boiled <alive> in its mother's milk.* Such is "bad faith"; *mauvise foi.

Our marvelously insightful redactor had to be both savvy and careful in putting this matter before us.

****

****

Keep in mind as we go forward that in any case "Rabbi Ishmael" made an attempt to "de-dietize" the significance of these thrice-articulated mandates by metaphorizing the "Threeness trope" of our thrice-articulated mandate so as to point to the three major geographical sites by which God and the Jewish People entered into the Covenant.

*****

Rabbi Elisha ben Abuya ((later referred to as "Rabbi Ishmael **ben Elisha**")) was committed to what today we might call the "plain-sense" of Scripture. The "plain sense" of Scripture should be taken as the default norm for understanding just about everything in Scripture (and as well as the basis for possible translations). In this vein, please understand that a "plain sense" reading or a "plain sense" translation is to be **clearly distinguished from what is called, these days, a "literal" reading or translation**. Even so, **sometimes** a word or phrase in our Scripture **must** be treated, both in reading and in translations, in a "literal" manner to as to get a first approximation of what is written; at that point one should then revert to a "plain sense" understanding of the Scripture portion.

And then there is the situation of the thrice-articulated mandate.

We already have the answer with "Rabbi Elisha's" daring-but-true opening in response to the thrice-articulated mandate as the opening of his -- "Rabbi Elisha's" -- return to being the Head of the *Beit ha Midrash*.

In other words, when a mandate such as the thrice-articulated mandate is deployed there must be a suspicion to the effect that either a literal and/or "plains-sense" interpretation ***radically misses the point***. Scripture here is prompting the reader to break through the surface meaning. To relegate this totally idiosyncratic ----- thrice articulated and not supported in all three cases by its immediate context ----- to the level of a merely dietary mandate is to (and I mean this literally) blind; perhaps willfully blind. SHAME!

****

****

****

****

****

POSTSCRIPT

A SENTIMENTAL JOURNEY

Matthew

Prolog:

The genesis of the New Testament is one filled with Shame and "*bad faith.*" Presenting Yeshu as a founder of Christianity is akin to making a square circle. But there is one substantial passage which, so to speak, rises to the level of true revelation:

One flew over the Cuckoo's Nest.

This saved text is one of the VERY few true portrayals of Yeshu in the Synoptics; and this portrayal was both real and substantial. <<<<The

"Fourth" Gospel is another story. It is VERY layered and layered in two major ways. But for the adept reader one can distinguish the grain from the dross.>>>>

Of the Synoptics *Mathew's* Gospel generally, is the least Christian-esque. And whether it is any of the Synoptics or the Fourth Gospel one thing is for sure: Yeshu would be **embarrassed -- indeed he would be pissed off --** at how he was mostly portrayed in all four Gospels. The Fourth comes closest by virtue of its idiosyncratic genesis; but -- as with the other three -- Yeshu is grossly misconstrued even in the accounting which is, on one level, the most SEMITIC of all the Yes, Yes, Yes. There are Huge incongruities of and between all four Gospels; but, in varying ways, ALL of the Gospels largely misconstrue Yeshu. But <again>:

One flew over the Cuckoo's Nest

In other words: This small vignette managed to keep at bay the cloudy and egregiously false ways in which Yeshu is portrayed, especially in the Synoptics.

*****

Yeshu was **not** founding a New religion. If he could, somehow, read the four Gospels, he would get a lawyer to outline just how **HUGE** was the gross negligence --- in various ways in each of the Gospels -- relative to Truth. Yeshu was born a Jew; Yeshu lived as a Jew; and Yeshu died as a Jew. Case closed.

But lo and behold!: There is this one episode -- this one from Matthew's Gospel -- which is genuine. Genuine because it unambiguously reveals **Yeshu's total grounding in Judaism**. Even his sparring with the Pharisees is quintessentially JEWISH. But what we have here is the most graphic portrayal of what Yeshu was really about.

So let us turn to Matthew 15: 21 – 28.

A Revealing Sentimental Journey.

Yeshu left that place and withdrew to the region of Tyre and Sidon

Was he alone on this journey? An other Synoptic seems to imply that this was a sentimental journey made alone. And such would be credible scenario given the reason for the journey in the first place. Our passage from *Matthew*, however, indicates that some of Yeshu' closest followers accompanied him to this part of Israel. When there is a discrepancy between and/or among the Synoptics, my bet would always go the Gospel of *Matthew*. Take away the noise of the redactors from the second century ce of this Gospel, and one has a fairly reliable accounting of this troubled man who lived and died as a Jew.*

*. *Coitus Interruptus*?????? Or just the opposite???????
****
****
****
****

"--- **a fairly reliable accounting of this troubled man** ----"?????
Not so quick. The Gospel of Matthew ((whether it be from Matthew straight out or by redactors who tried their best to expunge from "the Record" the profound Jewishness of Yeshu)) has its severe limitations. For the record:
What about the condensation of a three year ministry into one year which allowed

the Synoptics to suppress the fake "resurrection" orchestrated by Yeshu and his younger companion?
And even worse; let it be further probed:
The egregious suppression of that most horrible-and-amazing false "Resurrection" of Lazarus.
Everybody alive in Jerusalem (and much of beyond of Jerusalem) came to have some knowledge of that fake resurrection about a week before the crucifixion of Yeshu. But you would never have guessed it if you only read the Synoptics.
Of COURSE some set of redactors decided to ignore that chapter of Yeshu's ministry in all three of the Synoptics. And they almost got away with it. But as -- shall we call it fate? -- there was that late-found document <<<albeit written less than ten years after Yeshu died>>> accounting of Yeshu based on Rabbi El'azar's accounting soon after the crucifixion. This accounting was down to earth: The good; the bad; and the ugly. Although it was written only about five <at most> years after the Crucifixion, it was the last Gospel to be "found," so to speak. Why? The writer of that production lived to be 89ce and did not share it with his Jewish partners at Yavne.
Many of his colleagues -- even though most of them had voted for the ex-communication -- were sobered up with the news that El'azar was on his death-bed. Even his enemies came to sense that they had treated the **greatest** *Halakhist* very shabbily. And, indeed, Rabbi Joshua, after El'azar died, pulled some strings with Rabbinic Officaldom. The

ex-communication was officially rescinded. What do I say? **SHAME!**; too little too late.

*****

Back to the manuscript. Rabbi El'azar had left it to his son who eventually sold it. Over time it came into the ownership of one of the relatively early "Fathers of the Church." In its original form it was too hot to handle given the direction of the emerging Christian Religion. Indeed these early promoters wanted to burn the manuscript. But there was SO MUCH MORE in the document about Yeshu and El'azar which HAD to be saved. What they did do was to *gerrymander* (so to speak) the passages which "shouted-out" that this document was a document FOR JEWS AND ONLY FOR JEWS. Further, It was a document wherein there was a **major** tension, rivalry, and, sometimes, hatred which obtained between Yeshu <and his followers> and the leaders of the Pharisaic Sect.

In the document, Yeshu is portrayed as viciously condemning the Pharisaic invention of the Oral Torah; and in turn the Pharisees --- when Yeshu went "overboard" during these confrontations -- the Pharisaic rejoinder usually came in the form of castigating the "missing father" and, as well, castigating the "Magdala" who was the mother of Yeshu.*

> *. {The tension between Yeshu and the members of the Pharisaic Sect was real. And indeed, on at least one occasion, members of the Pharisaic Sect picked up stones and threw them towards Yeshu who high-tailed into

the background forest. After all, the matters engaged here "cut to the quick."

But even with this level of acrimony the interchange was truly an **IN<u>TRA</u>**change <u>within</u> Judaism Itself. Most Christians claim the mantle of Yeshu. But the real bottom line is that -- had Yeshu lived to see the origins of Christianity (and he did NOT) -- he would be **embarrassed <u>FOR</u>** them; and, correlatively he would snicker at some of the outrageous presumptions of this wacky spin-off. In other terms one might say that the acrimony between Yeshu's <u>SCRIPTURE-CENTERED</u> way of being Jewish ----- compared to in contrast, the more complex Pharisaic Sect which acknowledged, of course, Scripture but also those putative Oral Torah mandates **<u>----- at that time, BOTH ways stayed well within possible parameters of Judaism</u>**. Indeed, even today, these both accountings of Judaism fall under the larger meaning of "Judaism" and (perhaps more important) **<u>both</u>** are ways of "being-Jewish" and are well within the parameters of "being Jewish."

In contrast, that emerging "Christian" *min* was a vector to a **constructed** Yeshu who, allegedly, started a new religion which, from the Jewish perception, extended ---- and largely left behind --- the milieu and ambience which allows for Jewishness in the first place.}

****
****
****
****
****
****
****

Picking up the Thread again.
The Fathers of the Church decided to smooth out from the El'azar manuscript what would be helpful for the emerging Christian Church, when possible; and to "bend" the account in such a way that the text was gerrymandered to support a kind of "Yeshu" more in the mode of "Jewish-lite" ------------ which, of course was ridiculous. Good, bad, or ugly (or all three) Yeshu was Jewish through and through; he was born of a Jewish mother; he live as a Jew and practiced as a Jew; and he died as a Jew. The true Yeshu has no context at all except of **being Jewish**.
Those Fathers also interjected into the text a fair amount of what later would be called Anti-Semitism. Those "Fathers" already knew about Saul/Paul's "letters" and the Anti-Semitism thereof.
So what did they do? They took what they wanted <which includes the Anti-Semitism> and built on it while dismissing the portions of the manuscript which were too Jewish for "the Fathers."

And what about the fake Resurrection? These "artists" were very clever. They orchestrated from this "Fourth-Gospel's" original version (i.e., the fake Resurrection of Rabbi El'azar) and turned it into a miraculous Resurrection which, in this fakery, was the <putative> high-point of Yeshu's ministry!!!!!!????? What happened to **TMA**?????

****
****
****

And then there was this. Yeshu has no context except for his Judaism. That having been acknowledged, there was a streak in Yeshu which, today, we would call a *narcissistic disorder.* His *mamzer* status plagued him far more than one would ordinarily guess. He carried within his soul a great lust for being special. In this vein he carried within himself *the missing father.* It is no surprise that Yeshu came up with:

THE FATHER AND I ARE ONE

It is also no surprise that that the Pharisaic faction counted such a claim as blasphemous.

Indeed, in one of the Gospels there was a scene (prior to the fake resurrection by about two weeks) wherein Yeshu -- on the edge (some would say OVER the edge) -- ratcheted up his orientation to say something which most Jews would count as BLASPHEMY. Listen for yourself.

The Pharisees were taunting Yeshu with regard to the fact that he was a *mamzer* and had never came face-to-face with his father. The Pharisees kept up the drumbeat. They claimed Abraham as their Father and then asked "*WHO IS <u>YOUR</u> FATHER?* That hurt bad. Compulsively Yeshu rejoined with a statement which clearly smacks of *BLASPHEMY.*

To wit:

THE FATHER AND I ARE ONE

His Pharisaic audience was enraged. They picked up rocks and threw them at Yeshu. Yeshu quickly retreated to a forest area on a hill. (((((Indeed, there was only one other blasphemy worse than what Yeshu had just said.)))))

****
****
****
****
****

*****

OF COURSE all of this got back to Caiaphas. For the first time Caiaphas was no longer so sure that "The Plan" would prevail. On the contrary it seemed prudent to scotch "The Plan" altogether. But he decided he would make a final decision: a face-to-face with Yeshu.

A NOTE:

Yeshu was quick to viciously condemn the Pharisaic invention of the Oral Torah; and in turn the Pharisees --- when Yeshu went overboard in his nasty way of castigating the "Oral Torah" *imbroglio* --- were quick to castigate Yeshu not only on the plane of the *Halakha*, but also on another plane. I am speaking of the "magical" <<and, at times, the fraudulently "magical">>. This was anathema for most Jews and certainly anathema for the Pharisaic Sect. Keep this in mind.

*****

And there is one more thing.

We have already seen that the "Fathers of the Church" were VERY SKEPTICAL relative to this *ur*--manuscript. There is a HUGE difference between

sectarian strife *within* Judaism and -- by contrast -- the God-awful strife between Judaism and those "Fathers of the Church."
Yes. There was some strife -- even hate -- of and between the sectarian movements *within* Judaism. But there was ***a very <u>different</u>, and hate-ridden*** dynamic when the "Fathers of the Church" collectively took it upon Itself to judge the soil/the soul/the spirit of **<u>being</u>** Jewish.

The "Fathers of the Church" lived and breathed something radically different from **<u>being Jewish</u>**. In other words the reality was that "The Fathers" ***just-didn't-get-"it"*** at all.

And there is another dynamic at work. The "Fathers of the Church" were very educated and intelligent. But Jewish intellectuality was quite different from the intellectuality of the "Fathers of the Church." And that's OK.
Good, bad, or indifferent the "spiritual air" of Judaism was not the "spiritual air" of The Fathers of The Church. And that's OK
BUT HERE ARE THE THREE MAJOR POINTS:
a). *a circle will never be a square. Period. Yes. They are both geometrical figures just as the Fathers of the Church breath the same air which is breathed by Jews.* **But a square which is really a square cannot be a circle and a circle cannot be a square; ever.** And that's OK as well, unless one of the parties insists that, say, the Jewish circle must become a Christian square.
b). That last observation reveals another deep chasm between being a Christian and being Jewish. Except for just a small errancy on the cusp of the "common era" Judaism is not a proselytizing religion. Judaism is open to those, who in good faith, want to be counted as Jewish. But Judaism

does not **seek** converts. <<And don't be surprised if it turns out to be the case that some putative squares were and are really circles.>>
c). And, unfortunately, there is this:

Those Fathers also interjected into the text a fair amount of what later would be called 'Anti-Semitism.' In the final analysis Anti-Semitism was born with Christianity.* Those "Fathers" already knew about Saul/Paul's "letters" and the Anti-Semitism thereof. And what did they do? They made the "Letters" of Saul/Paul endemic to the Christian Bible!!!!! This was the true birth of Anti-Semitism. Yes; *Beit Yisrael* in the many centuries prior to the emergence of Christianity had enemies ---fierce and with much bloodshed. But all of that is bloodshed over land and such and not Anti-Semitism. It took the New Testament to birth Anti-Semitism.

> *. {OF course there were enemies of *Beit Yisrael* in the millennium prior to the "common era"; indeed fierce and vicious enemies. Case in point: The utter destruction of the Northern Kingdom in 721 and the utter loss of the "Ten Tribes" of the Northern Kingdom. These things were, of course, horrendous. But in fact there was nothing *"anti-Semitic"* about this tragedy. The whole course of history is filled with terrible warfare. But the tragedy of 721 was not Anti-Semitic. The Assyrians were in the ascendancy. They acted the same way with other Peoples and other Lands.
>
> Anti-Semitism is different. It is an abnormal fixation on Jews AS Jews. This did not come into being as a function of winning territory, etc., etc. No. Anti-Semitism is not any of that. Anti-Semitism is a fixated hatred

which -- if it could be "successful" -- would be a lusting in the service of annihilating all the Jews. Anti-Semitism is an irrational fixation on JEWS AS JEWS. And this phenomenon came into being with and by the emergence of the Christian religion.*

> *. {{I went out of my way in the early part of this production to point out that, ever since the *HOLACAUST* Christians, by and large, have freed themselves from Christianity's two millennia of Anti-Semitism. Further, on the average, Christians these days are very supportive of the State of Israel, the Homeland of the Jews. Nonetheless, the TWO MILLENNIA of Christian-based Anti-Semitism should not be swept under the rug. And yes, over those millennia there were Judeo-file Christians who were subjected to horror and death for speaking up for the Jews. They should be celebrated and they are celebrated in Jewish circles. But the numbers were pitiful. Less than one-tenth of one percent who spoke up over those two Christian millennia <prior to the Holocaust>. And of that one-tenth of one percent of those who spoke up publically (and some took action) would parse out as one-tenth of one tenth.}}
>
> }

Codicil to the above.
That was then; this is now.

****

****
****

What about the fake Resurrection? These "artists" were very clever. They orchestrated from this "Fourth-Gospel's" original version (i.e., the fake Resurrection of Rabbi El'azar) and turned it into a miraculous Resurrection which, in this fakery, was the putative high-point of Yeshu's ministry.
****
****
****
****

FINALLY!: Continuing on with ***the sentimental journey***:
The missing father. The ache which would never heal. The Sidonian archer who had been drafted into the Roman Army.
A small military contingent, including the Archer in question, was deployed for a short period of time in Nazareth. His name was Pantera. Then there is the young and beautiful maiden <but hardly a virgin>. Should be called it rape? Yes and No. If rape means forcible intercourse with a maiden who actively resists the man's onslaught, then this was not a rape. Is it a rape if the maiden passively acquiesces to a soldier in the Roman Army ((recall, here, that the whole of *Yisrael* was under the onerous Roman Occupation))? A case could be made to the effect that such was a rape anyway since the HUGE Power equations radically favored the soldier.
But then again, this was Miriam Magdala <"Hairdresser">. It was a 'profession' which was, to say the least, looked upon -- especially in Nazareth -- askance.

And there is this as well. Yeshu -- the product of **this** amorous encounter was clearly the favorite of all of Miriam's many children.
But of course there were would other children. First and foremost there was Joseph (brought up from the extended family in Bethlehem) into the picture rapidly as an attempt to deflect away from the fact that Yeshu was a *mamzer*. And then Joseph rose to the occasion and gave to Miriam two more children, one of them a female. And then by Joseph's brother, Cleopas, after Joseph died, who produced for Miriam two more brothers and one sister
Miriam doted on the first-born child. The truth was that this first-born turned out to be the handsomest of all the male progeny. It was her pride and joy. Fatherless and a doting Mother. It is, in effect, an archetype. In any case, how could Miriam feel this way if it were a forceful rape (or for that matter that non-forcible <<i.e., an acquiescing without a struggle meaning of rape>>?). Indeed, she most probably felt lucky to have her first progeny from a handsome soldier. And indeed, Yeshu was taller than the other male progeny. By the standards of Nazareth her first-born surely stood out.
The Sidonian Archer.
****

Continuing on -- finally!!!!! --:
Yeshu is approached by a Canaanite woman who claims that her daughter is tormented by an evil spirit. Yeshu ignored her. She then intruded on the small group of Yeshu's followers to get Yeshu to do something about this woman who was causing a commotion. They in turn prodded Yeshu to do something about the situation.
What Yeshu says here should be taken to heart for those who seek the truth about Yeshu: *His* ***innate***

Jewishness; and as well: what his true self-imposed mission was all about. To his disciples he makes it clear what his calling is about:

I WAS SENT ONLY FOR THE LOST SHEEP OF ISRAEL

*****

The Canaanite woman was persistent. She threw herself down and knelt before Yeshu and she begged for her daughter' sake. Even then Yeshu was resistant. Indeed, Yeshu was insulting to this frenzied woman. Listen:

IT IS NOT JUST TO TAKE THE CHILDREN'S FOOD AND TOSS IT TO THE HOUSE DOGS

This woman -- who for some reason thought this man could help her deranged daughter <perhaps foolishly> -- was very clever. She simply accepted the taunt which Yeshu had threw to her (and for that matter her daughter); she accepted that she was but a Gentile; she cleverly accepted that, being a Gentile, she was, in effect, one of those "house dogs." Her response to Yeshu's clear slur on the Gentiles was one of validating that she WAS JUST A GENTILE; and she said:

Ah yes! But even house-dogs can eat the scraps that fall from their master's table.

Yeshu now understood that he had been checkmated by this clever Gentile. He admired her persistence. Yeshu's response, however, was not a promise:

May your wish be granted

*****

Predictably, a redactor of this passage offered a final soothing comment:

And from that moment her daughter was well again.

(maybe; maybe not)

***** ***** ***** ***** *****

What we can take from this vignette are the forceful words by Yeshu and put forth by Matthew without ambiguity:

IT IS NOT JUST TO TAKE THE CHILDREN'S FOOD AND TOSS IT TO THE HOUSE DOGS

These are the words of Yeshu. Gentiles, in his view, were "house-dogs." What might be referred today the "Boyarin wish-fulfillment patrol" and other such groups who totally misunderstand what Yeshu was up to. To be sure, he was both a tortured (even to the point of self-hatred) and erratic Jew. But first, last, and always a Jew. No more; no less. Once again the sole goal of his self-appointed ministry; let it sink in:

I WAS SENT ONLY FOR THE LOST SHEEP OF ISRAEL

IT IS NOT JUST TO TAKE THE CHILDREN'S FOOD AND TOSS IT TO THE HOUSE DOGS

****

****

****

Turn now to Chapter Eight of the Fourth Gospel <8:13 -- 58>. Yes, the "Greek Gospel" (the fourth

Gospel). But scholars have verified that if you strip the Gospel of its Greeky aura,* we might be in the company of the most accurate portrayal of Yeshu's ministry, life, and death. Some have maintained that the '*ur*'-Fourth Gospel was written by the one who perhaps knew Yeshu more than anyone else. I am speaking of El'azar. Stripped of the Hellenic overlay of this Gospel (--- an overlay brought to this *ur*-text almost a century posterior to when this "Gospel" <albeit such would NOT be the meaning as it was originally written ---) is the most Semitic of all the Gospels. El'azar came from a wealthy and influential family in Bethany. He was well known by both the Roman officials and by High Jewish officials. By virtue of his family wealth and status, doors were opened to El'azar which most of the followers of Yeshu could not even aspire to. It was through this avenue that the lowly Nazarene Yeshu came to be received in "higher society."

****
****
****
****
****

****
****
****
****
****

SHUVU

It is you and it is me who must <u>SHUVU</u>. Indeed it is virtually the whole of* Beit Yisrael *who must <u>SHUVU</u>. Scripture-centricity is

the key for all, including Scripture-centricity for the determining of the Halakha. *As for the putative Oral Torah* halakhot *there is but one solution: Degrade those putative Oral Torah* halakhot (and their ancillary supports) *to the level of* minhaggim. *AS it stands now those* minhaggim *have been graduated to a place* ((and a HUGE place at that)) *thereby dwarfing the true status of the* MITSVOT *of Scripture.*

The heart of Judaism still remains primarily with the Orthodox. But Orthodoxy has become not only "top-heavy"* {enough to sink the Jewish ship}; *this "top-heavy" burden* – A HUGE ONE AT THAT -- *is a major reality of what is terribly* wrong *with Orthodoxy. Much of Its spiritruality has become a* fetish. *It is not healthy. If nothing changes, nothing changes. And if nothing changes Orthodoxy ---- the very heart of Judaism ---- will disappear from our planet which means that* Judaism will disappear from our planet. *That is not God's Will.*

I have a suggestion. To the extent that it is possible (both now and in the future) let the woman have the power. They carry Jewish souls for nine months each time she conceives. They do not want a future for their children which is becoming a dead end.

If I am wrong on this, I am wrong. I may seem to be presumptuous (and maybe that's the whole of the story). On the other hand it is possible that a goy-boy convert <the halakhic credentials thereof which can be challenged> with thin observance sees things that others may not have yet seen. It is possible.

Culled from:

vaT meM felA

then

!UVUHS

****
****
****
****

Codicil on the treatment on Rabbi Elisha ben Abuya {later to be referred by "Rabbi Ishmael **ben Elisha**} with the showdown between Aqiba and his followers, here, and Rabbi Elisha, there:

Rabbi Elisha did the right thing by opening up of the session by the totally **de-*dietizing*** of the thrice-articulated mandate which was scheduled for the session. As you will remember he -- rather shockingly* -- did put forth as an opener which respected the "Threeness" of the thrice-articulated mandate. I am certain that you remember the scene:

Why is this law stated in three places? To correspond to the three covenants which the Holy One, blessed be He, made with Israel: One on Mount Horeb [at Exodus 24: 7 -- 8]; *one on the plains of Moab* [at *Deuteronomy* 29:11]; and one on Mounts Gerizim and Mount Ebal [*Deuteronomy* 29:11].

Again: You could have heard a pin drop.
There are several more things to be brought up at this point.

***** ***** ***** ***** *****

THE DAY THE MUSIC DIED

The whole point for Rabbi Elisha ben Abuya <later on as "Rabbi Ishmael ben Elisha"; "Rabbi Ishmael" for short> was to ***de-dietize*** the thrice-articulated mandate ((which, in fact, in the three offerings in Scripture had never been presented as a dietary matter; indeed, FAR from that)). Rabbi Elisha was alone in maintaining that the thrice articulated mandate:

Thou shalt not Seethe a Kid in its Mother's Milk was idiosyncratic. In all three deployments of this mandate the deployment was out-of-tune with the Scriptural context surrounding it. And this was the point <by our anonymous inserter>: To insert into Scripture something SO idiosyncratic so that readers would understand that the usual "plain sense" and or "literal" meanings are NOT germane. What is being presented in this thrice-articulated mandate is in the service of having an occasion to meditate on a most serious matter: **to recognize that we all can become monsters if**

<u>we let our humanity become diabolical.</u> <u>THIS IS THE IMPORT OF OUR THRICE ARTICULATED MANDATE.</u> This matter has been reviewed earlier in this production.
****

Of course the Pharisaic Sect had made this thrice-articulated idiosyncratic mandate central to their version of the *Halakha*. The Pharisaic Sect at Yavne more or less had a fetish with regard to dietary prohibitions. And they were quick to deploy this sacred thrice-articulated mandate in the service of, in matter of thinking, **valorizing** their deep proclivity to weight down the *Halakha* with dietary *halakhot*. After all, they could valorize that this thrice-articulated mandate was NOT from the Oral Torah, but from Scripture Itself. In other words, if one interpreted the thrice-articulated mandate AS a dietary mandate ***<u>AND ITS SOURCE WAS SCRIPTURE (AND NOT MERELY AN ORAL TORAH HALAKHA, THEN SUCH WOULD ENHANCE THE DIETARY ORIENTATION ENDEMIC TO THE PHARSAIC SECT</u>***.
All of that would be fine <u>except that the thrice-articulated mandate has nothing to do with dietary matters</u>. The kid boiling in its MOTHER' milk. The horrific implications transcends dietary matters. Rabbi Elisha understood this. And, as it would turn out, he payed an horrific cost for honoring Scripture's weighty **<u>warning</u>**.
*****

As was noted earlier Rabbi Elisha's two most gifted students were present in this session: Rabbi Josiah and Rabbi Jonathan. As we have seen above they had made it their business to be present with their beloved mentor. His two gifted students were not "affiliated" with the Yavne Community;

their home-base was in Southern Israel. They felt obligated to be present for the day when their mentor would once again lead the *Beit haMidrash* at Yavne after having going through the hell of finding his two sons -- one after another with but a short interim in between the deaths -- in his own household. A very mysterious development. There was, of course a mourning period; but beyond that it took a somewhat longer time before Rabbi Elisha could be strong enough to return to his position in the *Beit ha Midrash*.

****
****
****

Rabbis Josiah and Jonathan were shocked as much as anyone when Rabbi Elisha offered his opening of the session ***without any bow to the <<<claimed by the Pharisees*** <and possibly others who were not of the Pharisaic Sect>***>>>!!!*** As you will recall there was a period of total silence when Rabbi Elisha put forth the proposition that the thrice-articulated mandate called to mind the three major places and events wherein the *COVENANT* was articulated and celebrated.

His star pupil -- Rabbi Josiah -- had the honor on this special day when Rabbi Elisha returned as Head of the *Beit haMidrash* of the Yavne Community to offer the first commentary on Rabbi Elisha's opener. There was that long period of silence which interjected between Rabbi Elisha's amazing (some would call it outrageous) offering which was ***totally bereft of ANY dietary significance***. It fell to Rabbi Josiah to break the onerous silence.

Rabbi Josiah finally spoke up. As it would turn out his offering --- <starting only AFTER the *generic* first part of Josiah's offering which was not involved in any dietary import> --- concerning the thrice-articulated mandate from Scripture was not at all disposed to ignore the dietary significance. He covered a number of matters which launched a bevy of dietary considerations with follow-up which continued <<albeit, after a while>> rather smoothly for the first session <which ended six lines from the top of page 488>.

<u>HOWEVER!:</u>

Rabbi Josiah offered -- before he had set in motion a dietary interpretation of the thrice-articulated mandate -- a consideration which dealt with a kind of indirect rejection of Rabbi Elisha's <<<amazing? Deep? Revelatory? Or just outrageous? <in context> >>> interpretation and the offering thereof which opened the discussion. To wit: the offering of Rabbi Elisha: *the three sacred places wherein God and the Jewish People made their Covenant.*

Herewith Rabbi Josiah's <Rabbi Elisha greatest mentee> opening offering:

Rabbi Josiah said <with reference to Elisha's stunning opening:

> *As regards the first (part) of this passage* ((i.e. the "Covenantal" interpretation of the thrice-articulated mandate)) ----- *it is the very first statement of the subject, And first statements <u>cannot be deployed for any special interpretation.</u>**
> *The second statement was said to meet the following argument*: <<a set of articulations, involving the "three-trope" orientation which, of course, is in tune with the thrice-articulated mandate ***on a dietary plane.***>>

Rabbi Josiah did not use scathing language in that initial first statement of <u>his</u> offering. But it is clear that the mentee is castigating his mentor for his "offering" ***which had NO dietary significance***.

{{{One might make the claim that Rabbi Josiah was blindsided by Elisha's extraordinary offering; in any case Rabbi Josiah ignores the non-dietary offering

by Elisha in favor of engaging the matter as a dietary matter.}}}
Whether or not Elisha's offering was a stroke of genius or something stupid can be argued either way. But to my mind it was Rabbi Elisha who was attuned to the true significance of the thrice-articulated mandate. Even his two mentees seemed blind to what he, Elisha, had put on the table.
*****
At this point we are, textually, from roughly the second half of page 486 (Lauterbach pagination, of course) to the second deployment of the thrice-articulated mandate towards the second time when the thrice articulation was put forth:

Thou shalt not Seethe a Kid in its Mother's milk.

((Once again, we are reminded that this has little to do with dietary matters and everything to do with the gross perversions we humans are capable of.))
*****

THE DAY THE MUSIC DIED

We are now engaged with one of the most momentous passages in ALL of Jewish literature.
It came down to *mano a mano*: Rabbi Elisha ben Abuya and Rabbi Aqiba ben Yosef.
Let's be clear: The Second session started on page 488 with:

*Thou Shall Not Seethe a Kid in its Mother's Milk**

****
****
****

*. RECTIFICATION:
In a previous production:

felA vaT meM

then

!UVUHS

I was unthoughtful. At one time of my ignorance I maintained that the presence of Rabbis Josiah and Jonathan at the *Beit haMidrash* at Yavne as per page 486 of Lauterbach's *Mekhilta* was a ruse orchestrated by Rabbi Aqiba. Doubtlessly my overall negative feelings concerning Rabbi Aqiba had something to do with this admission. When I first engaged this text for the writing of the book you are now reading I presumed that, nefariously, Aqiba had orchestrated the false presence of these two main mentees of Rabbi Elisha ben Abuya <aka "Rabbi Ishmael ben Elisha"//"Rabbi Ishmael" for short> as a way of showing these two mentees of Rabbi Elisha as being not so sharp as what one would presume if one were a major mentee of "Rabbi Elisha ben Abuya" aka "Rabbi Ishmael ben Elisha."

I was straight-out wrong.

In this production I was quick to note that both of these mentees WERE INDEED IN THE FLESH for the return of Rabbi Elisha as Head of the *Beit haMidrash* Yavne.

That having been said, it is noteworthy that -- especially in the case of Rabbi Josiah -- these two gifted mentees "failed" to rise to the offering concerning the thrice-articulated mandate by stripping the thrice-articulated mandate of ANY dietary weight. Doubtlessly they too were shocked by the ***covenantal*** interpretation of that thrice-articulated mandate. Indeed, these two mentees -- perhaps fearing that they would lose face with all the Rabbis in attendance who -- excepting the returning Rabbi Elisha -- would most certainly insist on a **dietary** interpretation of the thrice-articulated mandate.

Enough said.

But not really. *wiki* puts forth the following concerning Rabbis Josiah and Jonathan:

a).

Josiah is frequently mentioned in the Mekhilta *together with Jonathan.* ***All of their differences concerned ONLYINTERPRETATIONS OF BIBLICAL PASSAGES; NOT HALAKHOT.***

And b).

Rabbi Tavi said in the name of Rabbi Josiah:

---- *the* HalaMekhiltakha *in both cases follows the more lenient authority.*

But of course. What else would one expect from the star student of "Rabbi Elisha ben Abuya" aka "Rabbi Ishmael ben Elisha." Most certainly these two offerings are truthful. The two citations are in synch on these two matters. But, as we have just seen, neither of these two scholars would follow the daring interpretation put forth by Rabbi Elisha (who, in the *Mekhilta* is referenced as "Rabbi Ishmael").

****

****

****

****

****

There must have been something like a "caucus" orchestrated by the Pharisaic Sect during the break. Rabbis Joshua and Aqiba were the two catalysts. It was determined that Rabbi Aqiba would be the front man. He would go *mana a mana* with Rabbi Elisha. {{{as the *Coup* marched on, it would Rabbi Joshua who would take the lead in

deposing Rabban. Finally Rabbi Joshua would also take the lead in the ex-communicating of Rabbi El'azar ben Hurcanus. The three giants would be deposed. Yes, there was still the matter of Gamliel and his hereditary position. Rabbis Aqiba and Joshua offered a compromise wherein the young Shimon bar Yokhai would hold the hereditary position for one week out of four weeks while Gamliel would hold the hereditary for three weeks each month. But in any case the power was with Aqiba and Joshua. After Rabbi Joshua had a "sit-down" with Gamaliel it was clear that the "new regime" was going to prevail. Gamaliel agreed without reservation.
The (ugly) *Coup* within the Yavne Community.}}}
But we are getting ahead of ourselves. The immediate goal was to break the spirit of "Rabbi Elisha ben Abuya" who had suffered the deaths of his two sons.
****
****
****

The "NOES!" lose big time. Pages 488 through 492. I count seven times wherein Lauterbach follows this or that "NO" with an exclamation mark. Rabbi Elisha was already weakened. By the time of the second session there was no issue of any "resurrection" of the three 'covenants' by which *Beit Yisrael* and "The Holy One, blessed be He" consummated the Covenant. It was clear from the first reaction to that surprise offering by Rabbi Elisha <back in the first session> concerning the Covenant that his hope to *de-dietize* the thrice-articulated mandate was simply not going to be sustained. "Majority Rules." And in this particular matter "Majority Rules" **decimated** TRUTH.
*****

In this second session (of the Noes) it was Rabbi Aqiba who brought up what are spurious arguments concerning the thrice-articulated mandate. Rabbi Aqiba -- who sensed some weakness in Rabbi Elisha -- shot out spurious possibilities which he claimed would sustain the putative prohibition for mixing meat and milk in cooking. The verbal assaults were one after another. They were incredibly WEAK offerings; offerings which even Aqiba should have understood as weak <<<or baiting Rabbi Elisha with outrageously weak offerings as a way of saying: *WE (THE PHARISEES) ARE GOING TO WIN IRREGUARDLESS OF ANY OFFERINGS PROFFERRED).* In any case, for Aqiba, truth was not the goal. Getting under the skin of Rabbi Elisha was the goal. Indeedd WINNING was the goal.
It was clear to Elisha that he was not involved in a true *halakhic* discussion. And there was this to consider: The true holy and sacred import of the thrice-articulated mandate received no recognition. All the challenges to Elisha **presupposed** ((i.e., a RUDE begging the question)) that the issue was ONLY A DIETARY matter.

But----- ((and the whole two sessions seemed to weaken him; after all it was not so long ago that, mysteriously, his only two children died -- one after the other with just a small time in between)) ---
-- Elisha would vociferously respond **NO!** to the off-center offering visited upon him by Aqiba. In turn, Elisha competently revealed the weaknesses of Aqiba's arrows; and not only that. More to the point Elisha countered with sharp and **halakhically significant** responses showing, in each challenge, ***to the effect that --- extrinsic factors being accounted for -- there was NO IMPEDIMENT,***

Halakhically, for the mixing of milk and meat in cooking.

In other words, the Head of the *Beit haMidrash* (i.e., Rabbi Elisha ben Abuya) by default would now have to address the thrice-articulated mandate **AS A DIETARY MANDATE**.
*****

In point of fact, as we shall see, Rabbi Elisha, will have to make his "fall-back" position be one which derives from that radically faulty position endemic to the Pharisaic Sect at Yavne that "milk and meat" cannot be cooked together.
In fact Elisha, as we shall see below, **does make a case that ----- extrinsic variables** <such as a carcass, for example, "which died of itself" would, *just by that fact*, thereby precluding such a carcass to be cooked> taken into consideration, **-----** ***there is in fact NO prohibition for mixing meat and milk to be cooked together***. Listen to Rabbi Elisha:

PROEM:
Now that we have addressed the **extrinsic** variables which would disallow the mixing of meat and milk together, we find that there is in fact no prohibition for cooking the mixture; or eating the cooked mixture; or selling the cooked mixture.
Listen:
Rabbi Elisha speaking (pages 491 – 492):

> ***ONLY meat and milk are forbidden to be cooked together; but all other prohibited things mentioned in the Torah are not! For the following argument would be advanced:*** (to wit):
> ***If it is forbidden to cook together meat with milk*** {{along with eating the mixture and/or selling the mixture}} ***ALTHOUGH EACH ONE BY ITSELF IS PERMITTED TO BE COOKED AND EATEN, IS***

IT NOT LOGICAL THAT PROHIBITED THINGS MENTIONED IN THE TORAH,* EACH OF WHICH BY ITSELF BY ITSELF IS FORBIDDEN, SHOULD **SURELY BE FORBIDDEN TO BE COOKED TOGETHER?????**

Therefore it says: "You shall not seethe the kid <in its mother's milk; etc."

Only meat and milk are forbidden to be cooked together WHILE ALL OTHER PROHIBITED THINGS ARE NOT?????!!!!!

The cutting irony is exquisite. Of course "Rabbi Elisha" understood by now that he was going to lose the matter involved. But he was no longer addressing the hell-bent audience who would be -- by "*majority rules*" (but certainly not by "truth") --- "victorious" on this fateful day.

OF Course, "Rabbi Elisha" understood that the Pharisees at Yavne were hell-bent to maintain their sacred <to them> dietary understanding of this thrice-articulated mandate ***which intentionally cries out NOT TO BE UNDERSTOOD literally (or even according to the ordinary "plain sense" of the mandate).***

Rabbi Elisha understood that his counter-offering will be rejected and, even worse, this sacred mandate (when it is properly understood) will be demoted to a dietary caveat of the small-minded Pharisaic majority. He understands all that. What he is doing --- now that they are on the verge of a final vote -- is this: ***FOR THE RECORD***. Doubtlessly he prays for the time when this holy thrice-articulated mandate will be appreciated by others than himself.

*****

For most people, that would be the end of the story. But the love-affiar in the Pharisaic Sect <a

majority, by the way, at Yavne> with the Oral Torah (of which dietary laws are legion) will not happily cede the ground. Indeed this Tractate *Kaspa* of the *Milkhilta* is evidence of the Pharisaic fixation on dietary matters in general and upon the thrice-articulated mandate in particular.

On this rueful day, Aqiba "won." *Beit Yisrael* **LOST big-time**. It was the nature of Aqiba to WIN. It was a hollow win. The price is still HUGE--- *all the way to our own time* --- visiting pain and confusion century by century unto *Beit Yisrael*. It is a crime of the first order for the whole of *Beit Yisrael* <albeit the majority does not even see the criminality involved>. There is no blindness worse than those ***who WILL not see***.

*****

On that awful day: *BY HOOK OR BY CROOK THEY (the leaders of the Pharisaic Faction) DID WHATEVER NEEDED TO BE DONE TO SECURE THEIR ADOLESCENT FIXATION ON HAVING A MERE DIETARY INTERPRETATION OF THIS SACRED THRICE-ARTICULATE CAVEAT*

*****

Yes. As it will have turned out the Pharisees at Yavne "won" the battle with "Rabbi Elisha." But it was ----- ***AND IS STILL IS*** ----- a terrible defeat for Judaism as a whole over the millennia. We who are still alive are heirs of that defeat. It will have been **and is** a Pyric victory for the leaders of the Pharisaic Sect at Yavne. The matter got shamefully reduced to a mere diatary back and forth. In other words, the true matter was ignored; it wasn't even seen.

Sooner or later the community of *Beit Yisrael* will awaken to the cancer which has invaded into and settled into (for more than 1900 years) "The House of Israel."

****

****
****
****
****

SHUVU!

It is you and it is me who must SHUVU*. Indeed it is virtually the whole of* Beit Yisrael *who must* SHUVU*. Scripture-centricity is the key for all, including Scripture-centricity for the determining of the* Halakha. *As for the putative Oral Torah* halakhot *there is but one solution: Degrade those putative Oral Torah* halakhot (and their ancillary supports) *to the level of* minhaggim*. AS it stands now those* minhaggim *have been graduated to a place* ((and a HUGE place at that)) *thereby dwarfing the true status of the* MITSVOT *of Scripture.*

The heart of Judaism still remains primarily with the Orthodox. But Orthodoxy has become not only "top-heavy"* {enough to sink the Jewish ship}; *this "top-heavy" burden* – A HUGE ONE AT THAT -- *is a major reality of what is terribly* wrong *with Orthodoxy. Much of Its spirituality has become a* fetish*. It is not healthy. If nothing changes, nothing changes. And if nothing changes Orthodoxy ---- the very heart of Judaism ---- will disappear from our planet which means that* Judaism will disappear from our planet*. That is not God's Will.*

I have a suggestion. To the extent that it is possible (both now and in the future) let the woman have the power. They carry Jewish souls for nine months each time she conceives. They do not want a future for their children which is becoming a dead end.

If I am wrong on this, I am wrong. I may seem to be presumptuous (and maybe that's the whole of the story). On the other hand it is possible that a goy-boy convert <the halakhic credentials thereof which can be challenged> with thin observance sees things that others may not have yet seen. It is possible.

Culled from:

vaT_meM felA

then

!UVUHS

John W. McGinley
(aka; *Hullin*)

ISBN: 978-1-4575-4271-8
dog ear publishing

If the publisher will not sell the book then get in touch with me and I will send a copy to your organization (I will need an address) *gratis*.

*****

570-241-8074
35 West Street apt 2G
Farmingdale, NJ
07727

****
****
****

SHUVU!

O WAYWARD CHILDREN

H̲oos Akher

<he never left>

Do you get it yet? It is NOT Akher who must RETURN. The command-which-is-a plea.
Akher is not being stubborn. The great tension then and now (albeit it is largely a suppressed tension) is the status of the Oral Torah (and its accoutrements) *vis a vis* Scripture-centricity for the determining of the *Halakha*. The final anonymous editors had to use subterfuge phrasing in order to even get certain ideas and norms into the *Bavli* at all.
The Oral Torah comes from the Pharisees, not from God. Its weight on the *Halakha* (and its accoutrements) is terribly over-bearing. Basically, for the Orthodox, the Oral Torah has become a false god.
In contrast, for the rest of the non-Orthodox Sects of Judaism, it doesn't really matter. Lip service, here, is accorded to many things Jewish, but actual practice is rather thin and "surfacey": Pick and Choose.
*****
The Synogogues which are built -- especially in the Diaspera -- are grand edifices which are finding fewer and fewer "visitors" (that word is appropriate). Sects which never probe. Much is claimed, but only on the surface. In contrast over in Orthodoxy Land (whether in the Diaspera or in

Erets Yisrael) there is constant motion and activity withut true substance.
It can't go on like this. But it will. *If nothing changes, nothing changes.*
*****
"Modern Orthodoxy." Is that a solution? It certainly will not if it does not budge from the *de- facto* hegemony of the Oral Torah. Who is listening?
****
****

Shuvu

O My backsliding children.

Now keep in mind as well what has been articulated in this production:

The Oral Torah [and its paraphenelia] derives by Men by way of Human agency; The *Mitsvot* of our Scripture comes from Hashem by way of Human agency.

... /// ///

I call upon Heaven and Earth to witness against you this day: I have put before you life and death; blessing and curse.

Accordingly

CHOOSE LIFE!

That you and your offspring might live.
****

I address the Women of Jerusalem <"Jerusalem," here taking on the role of the part for the whole>. I am primarily addressing the Women of Orthodoxy. It falls to you. If you do not rise up with courage there will be the disappearance of the People. The time has come; the time is now. Rise up and do what it takes to *restore; return;* **SHUVU!**

Listen:

----- let it be done according to the Torah. For the matter rests upon you and we [your sons, daughters, and some husbands] are with you. BE STRONG AND ACT!

[*Ezra* 10: 3—4]
Suggestion:
Buy or Steal a copy of

lef<u>A</u> vaT meM
then
!UVUHS

Then read pages 338 339.
*****

On the Road of Connubiality
What follows is a pause.
The reading of Scripture is not akin to the reading of any other document including our precious *Bavli*, which itself, is a uniquely disquieting text. The reading of Scruipture involve us into the most intimate interchange between Hashem and *Beit YIsrael;* that interchange being Scripture Itself. At the same time the reading of Scripture involves us in the most scandalous love affair ever. It is the story of what appears to be a congenitally unfaithful wife here, and, there, a confused, hurting, and bitter husband who **returns** to her time after time. True. With each treacherous infidelity this husband visits pain -- both verbal and, so to speak, physical abuse to boot – on his faithless wife. But He is besotted with His erring wife. He loves her more than He loves Himself. He is a Fool. But He cannot help Himself.
And there is this as well: the wife, at root, is hopelessly -- desperately – in love with her husband. Yes. It is absurdly incongruous. Love hurts; and at the peak of intensity love is insane.

She is just as confused as her Husband as to why, time after time, she visits upon the Man she loves heartache without measure.

Obviously this cannot go on forever. The signs are all over the place that the Husband must soon abandon her even if it means certain death for the Husband. He is burnt out. He has no interest in another woman. They already live separately from each other. But in the early down He sneaked into her apartment while she was asleep. She of course had availed herself of her own pillow. He left a note on his unused pillow: *Honey! I love you and only you. Please listen:*

SHUVU!

****

****

There is a dueling duet all throughout the Bavli *involving a massive series of thrusts and counter-thrusts. The players are, on the one hand, the representatives of Rabbinic Officialdom. On the other hand there are the anonymous final editors who subterfugically deconstruct Rabbinic Officialdom in a glorious -- but seldom recognized -- attempt to convey to the right kind of reader the dreadful horror which was perpetrated on the "days" leading up to ((and as well as the "days" succeeding)) the "day of the oven of the Coiled Snake."* [[To be noted: these final anonymous editors had "fifth column" <so to speak> support within Rabbinic Officialdom <starting with Rabbi Judah>.]] *For that was the day which represents the tipping point by which the Pharisaic faction wrested control of the Movement from the founding fathers thereby making the Oral Torah normative for the Rabbinic Movement from the founding fathers at Yavne thereby making the Oral Torah normative* for the Rabbinic Movement.*

*. {In fact albeit not in theory}

****

Rabbi Judah ("Rebbi/Rebbe") was probably not even conceived at the time when the sessions in the *Beit ha Midrash* at Yavne, the notes of which would eventually (and with the guidance of Rabbi Judah much later) become "The *Mekhilta de* 'Rabbi Ishmael.'"

That guidance by Rabbi Judah ((including some inserts by his own hand here and there)) was a wondrous undertaking. It is the one sustained and intact production from the Yavne years* **before** the *Coup* from late 91 on up to the climax of 94. Indeed those tensions are well acknowledged in our *Mekhilta*, especially with regard to the sessions surrounding Tractate *KASPA* <in the second volume>.*

*. [

****

****

****

****

Deception and the Seal of Hashem.

The covenant is effectuated though deception. Truth is the Seal of Hashem. Both statements are true in all respects, at once. The paradigm for this paradox is that set of stories in *Genesis* dealing with Avram-becoming-Abraham; Sarah; Hagar; Isaac; Ishmael; Rebeqah; Esau; Jacob; Leah; Rachel; Dina; Judah, and Tamar. ((I am consciously leaving out of the series, here, the story of Joseph.))

Yes. Of course. It is obvious that the players in this series were masters and mistresses of deception. And the greatest of these is Jacob. But, while less recognized, Torah also makes it clear that the player *par excellence*, Hashem, is the very Master of Deception. Indeed, the deeper truth of Torah is that deception involving choice (human and Divine) is of a deeper and more radically significant

undercurrent of deception which no-one -- certainly not God and certainly not humans -- can or should escape. This whole nexus is exactly and precisely the story of how the Covenant came to be effectuated. It is story permeated with the sub-text to the effect that without the various human and Divine **deceptions** (both chosen and not chosen), the Covenant would simply NOT have been effectuated at all.
Yet it remains true that truth us the seal of Hashem.

Deception is the life-blood of truth.
Such is the deep and ***UNRESOLVABLE*** CHARACTER OF TRUTH. Honesty -- understood here as a life-long commitment to avoid and eradicate what cannot be avoided or eradicated (i.e., self-deception) -- is the midwife of truth. He who loves truth will be fighting this battle until her/his last shiver of consciousness (and -- who really knows -- even beyond).
Fine. But truth does not occur without life and life, of its very nature, does not occur on any level at all without deception. Any kind of life-form worth the writing of [[indeed, any life-form period]] runs on the very life-blood of deception.
Thus truth -- for it too is a life-form, after all -- runs on the very fuel to which it is committed to eradicate. There is simply no Hegelianesque (or **any other** "esque") outcome for this endemically ingrained tension which is life: for God and for Humans (and for all other life-forms). How we live the tension makes all the difference in the world. For, in the final analysis, life **IS** this tension ((consciously such or unconsciously such being a very secondary matter)) **and life itself** disappears without truth.

Truth and life have a symbiotic relation**<u>ing</u>** with each other. They both run on deception; but when truth disappears, life disappears. Whatever *olam ha-ba may* be or not be, this tension is there as well. It may be said that God, in His mercy, will only permit Torah scholars to enter *olam ha-ba*, for only Torah scholars, it would seem, would be happy there.

In all things submit to the Seal of Hashem.

****

****

****

****

****

****

****

Finnegan's Awakening

****

****

<u>EXERGUE</u>

<u>HSoDaQ</u>

<u>THE HOLY</u>

*****

A NOTE:

Doubtlessly Thrasyllus deserves great *encomia* for his gigantic work in generating accurate presentations of the authentic works of Plato's productions (and, just as importantly, showing that some productions claiming to be authored by Platonic were spurious).

Plato wrote much more than the thirty-five* dialogues which are known to have been from the "pen" of Aristocles from Athens. There are also thirteen "Letters" which are genuinely from the "pen" of Plato as well. But my more generic point is thus: He wrote more dialogues <and/or portions of dialogues which he never finished because he was not satisfied with what he was putting forth> than the thirty-five productions which he saved for posterity.

It is important to note that Thrasyllus -- ever the true "worshipper" of "Plato" -- did NOT organize the authentic productions of Plato <i.e., the ones which survived the burning of a number of productions by Plato himself>. On the contrary, true to his love of Plato, Thrasyllus did produce a new set manuscript-COPIES. But true to his love of Plato, Thrasyllus retained the order of the valid productions of Aristocles-from-Athens.

> *. {There is a **<u>true</u> <u>veneer</u>** of chronological orientation in Plato's organization of the thirty-six productions which were organized in nine "Tetrologies." The tetralogical organization largely falls in a *roughly* chronological sequencing. But Plato had no qualms about situationing what dialogues would be put forth in this or that Tetrology according to the subject matter of a given Tetralogy even if there were some sequencings which were not, strictly, chronological.
>
> In these matters, there are two salient productions which merit special consideration:
>
> *. i. {The fourth offering of the ninth Tetralogy was not a dialogue. This last production <<as per the tetralogical organization schema>> was a series of significant "definitions" orchestrated by Plato himself.}

ii. {Plato had no qualms about revising previously produced dialogues.
In this genre our dialogue, *Euthyphro** is significant. This dialogue was the opener for a series of Socrates-oriented dialogues wherein "Socrates" is clearly and directly portrayed as being alive even though Socrates was dead prior to ANY of the Platonic productions. Of course, we are referring to the sequence: *Euthyphro*; *Apology*; *Crito*; and *Phaedo*.**
iii). The deployment of "Socrates" subsequent to that first Tetralogy is mixed. Often enough "Socrates" is but an undeveloped "name-holder" for the dialogue in question. Then again "Socrates" is deployed in a more dynamic manner, especially if the scene of the dialogue incorporates into itself a remembered situation (e.g., as per *Republic*) wherein the role of Socrates was dynamic. And who could forget the "Young Socrates" in *Statesman*. Iv). And then, of course, a number of dialogues which simply eschews the presence of Socrates in favor of other figures for this or that dialogue, usually a late dialogue.

> *. {As we have seen, *Euthyphro* was a very early offering; but it was subsequently *"jimmied"* to allow for the final version of *Euthyphro* which was fairly late AND, ---- in such a revisionist presentation ----, philosophically and radically enhanced.}
>
> **. {The scene of The ur-*Phaedo* was portrayed as being in the prison itself on the actual day of Socrates' death. In a later and expanded version of the

Phaedo -- one finds the initiator of a CLEAR and unambiguous theory of 'Forms'.}

****
****
****
****
****

The EUTHYPHRO

The early rendition of this dialogue of the first Tetralogy was not nearly as long in its earliest rendition. It was not the best written production by Plato; but he made sure that this short-and-choppy dialogue would be the opening offering. However, as we shall see, the redactive hand of Plato ---- late in life but before he engaged the dialogues of the ninth Tetralogy ---- graduated this initially very short dialogue to a relatively LOADED accounting of things which even transcends those great dialogues, *Sophist* and *Parmenides*. Our expanded *Euthyphro* reaches out of the domain of Philosophy and, unconsciously, puts this dialog to the most important of all matters:

HSoDaQ

THE HOLY

*****

"ARISTOCLES" from Athens.

"PLATO" was his *nom de plume.*

In his subsequent Jewish incarnation his name was Joshua <'Yehoshua' if you wish>; the Joshua who had killed Moishe on Mount Sinai. He had been the faithful Lieutenant of Moishe. But when Moishe came down from his second ascent Moishe found that the Jewish encampment was out of control. Really out of control. That was bad enough. But ***worse*** was Moishe's reaction to those who mocked the "Great Leader" when Moishe had descended from the Mountain. His lofty pride was decimated. That very day he delegated the tribe of Levites to go from "house" <in a manner of speaking> to "house" in revenge (delegated by Moishe) slaughtering Mothers, Fathers, and Children. About **three thousand Jews were slaughtered that very day**. And he took no responsibility for what he had done.

Moishe went back up for his third ascent after He had talked to God in a most somber "Face to Face" back at the "Tent of the Meeting." This third ascent was posterior to the riot and posterior to what happened after the People had mocked him <i.e., the HUGE slaughter set in motion by Moishe>. In this third ascent (from which he never came down) he once again spoke to Hashem "Face to Face." This time he died. Joshua, surreptitiously, made sure of that. And, in effect, so did Hashem. In this last meeting between Hashem and Moishe Hashem went out of His way to alert Moishe to his forthcoming death:

NO ONE CAN SEE MY FACE AND LIVE

*****

The "shining" aura in and about the face (which was blinding) was a both a mask and metaphor whereby the redactor orchestrated a way by which leadership now had passed on to Joshua. This blinding shining Joshua was a military figure. The People knew Moishe (for better or for worse). Less was known of his Lieutenant, Joshua. There was a sense that this Lieutenant of Moishe would require much more discipline from the People if they were ever to return to their Homeland. It was also a way for the Scripture to say -- without actually saying in so many words -- that Moishe was dead. Joshua's shining descent from Sinai/Horeb was a way of announcing that Moishe was not coming down ever again.

*****

It was the *mazzal* of this Joshua which entered into the soul of Aristocles from Athens. The military figure had become a Philosopher.

****

****

<u>GENERIC DIMENSIONS ON PLATO</u>

35 saved dialogues; 13 "Letters"; and a piece called "Definitions."
36 saved productions ordered according to nine sets of four tetralogies. <"The Defnitions" were not dialogic; but "The Definitions" functions as the fourth entry of the ninth Tetralogy.

Euthyphro is the first dialogue of the first tetralogy. Two separable and not separable matters in this dialogue:
i). OSION: <u>Holiness/Piety</u> (i.e., the English of the Greek **OSION** allows for "Holy"/"Holiness" and "piety." This means that in the translation there are two English words which translate the one **OSION**. In English "piety" has several connotations and, given the context, "piety," is appropriate translation. A way of putting this is to suggest that when Euthyphro offers some accounting of OSION "piety" is the appropriate translation; so too, when Socrates responds to <u>Euthyphro's</u> accounting of OSION "piety"<at best!!!> is also the appropriate translation. On the other hand, when Socrates challenges Euthyphro to "up-grade" the meaning of OSION the meaning of OSION takes on the aura

of "The Holy." And, *a fortiori*, when Socrates speaks for himself (i.e., not only upgrading Euthyphro's meaning of OSION) it is clear that HOLY or HOLINESS are the appropriate translations of **OSION**.
The secondary translation is "Piety" which is used in this translation for the minor -- and less weightier – meaning**S** of **OSION**).
AND, ii). **DEFINITIONS** <what is the structure of a good definition?>. This is the other major matter of the dialogue. The two matters ------- "what is OSION?," here; and what constitutes a valid definition, there ------- fuse together. In other words, finding the primary meaning of OSION *eo ipso* is to steer the investigation of OSION with respect to the "causal factor" <which is a difficult matter> which makes OSION **to be** OSION.
*****
IRONY permeates the whole dialogue.
AND KEEP IN MIND, THIS DIALOGUE IS AN APORETIC DIALGUE.
****

The scene of the *Euthyphro*. Why are they there? Take note, carefully, the interchanges between what Socrates and Euthyphro say to each other. Background: religion centered around the Homeric Gods and Goddesses who, to say the least, were not Saints. Athens in transition. (War weary) The Golden Age of Athens is now gone. Transition. Sophistry. And the new kid on the block, the Spartans, in effect, ruled Athens.
****
****

I have availed for this meditation on **THE HOLY** the translation of *Euthyphro* from the "Internet Archives"; also the accounting from *CLASSICS*

OF WESTERN PHILOSOPHY (fifth edition; edited by Stephen Cahn); and finally: PLATO*: Complete Works*.
*****
In this production -- which is idiosyncratic -- the only matter being exhumed here from our dialogue is the accounting **OSION as** Holy/Holiness as *per* 10a ----- up TO AND INTO 11b and ending just before the "*But Socrates, ------"*
*****
Accounting now for this excerpt as indicated just above. It is the burning living center of *Euthyphro* by virtue of addressing the **CAUSAL FACTOR** in these matters.
Plato addresses this matter by giving quotidian examples of the **CAUSAL FACTOR**.
To wit: "something *being carried*" and, "*carryING*"; "something" *led*; and, *leadING*; *something; seen;* and, *seeing*.
Presumably the reader gets the gist.

Now we turn to something more germane: *something loved* ; and something *loving*.
What is the implication? Here we shall take just one of the examples:
Socrates speaking:

Tell me then whether the thing carried is a carried thing be-CAUSE it is being carriED; or for some other reason.

Euthyphro speaking:

No, that is the reason.

Keep in in mind.
*****
... ...
Continuing on:
Socrates speaking:
Is what I want to say clear, Euthyphro? I want to say if anything is being changed or *being affected in any*

*way, it is not being chang<u>ed</u> be**CAUSE** it is something chang<u>ed</u>, but rather it is something chang<u>ed</u> be**CAUSE** it is <u>being</u> chang<u>ed</u>; nor is it <u>being</u> affected be**<u>cause</u>** it is something affected, but, RATHER, it is affected be<u>cause</u> it is **<u>being</u>*** <u>affected</u>.

Do you not agree?

Euthyphro speaking:

I do

[THEN]:

Is something lov<u>ed</u> either something chang<u>ed</u> or affect<u>ed</u> by something?

Euthyphro speaking:

I do.

Socrates speaking:

*So it is in the same case as the things just mentioned; it is not being loved by those who love it because it is something loved; **<u>but, rather, 'the something' in question is something loved BECAUSE IT IS SUCH AS TO BE LOVED.</u>***

*****

After some distinctions are made by Socrates we find that, so far, the <u>NATURE</u> of Piety eludes us. However:

<u>Third proffered definition:</u> what all the Gods hate is impious, and what they all love is OSION; (and what some of them love and some of them hate is either both or neither). Socrates then gets Euthyphro to use this definition just put forth:

What all the Gods love is OSION, and the opposite, what they all hate, is impious

****
****

The above accounting has truth about it but it still lacks the full delineation of what might be referred to as THE CAUSAL FACTOR.

*****

Now it gets tough.

The last proffered definition does recognize the requirement that a good definition must be universal relative to the matter under discussion. However a universal which does not include A CAUSAL FACTOR is a limping definition. From the second half of the beginning of this text through the first half of page eleven, Plato puts forth the critical variables involved "the Causal Factor." Absent the causal factor in a definition the proffered definition is severely compromised.

Let us turn, then, to the significance of the **Causal Factor** relative to this matter of OSION.

<<Let us cheat here, a bit. Plato did not delineate a bunch of 'jargonesque' headings. That started with Aristotle. Plato eschewed such jargonesque applications. However, in the subsequent history of Philosophy, starting with his mentee, Aristotle, 'jargonsesque' articulations can sometimes help one to be precise. In our situation there are just two relevant articulations which are germane to Plato's attempt to catch the "essence" of a "causal factor" relative to exposing just what kind of causal factor leads to an understanding of what OSION **IS**.

The "making" cause <often referred to as the "efficient cause"> is easily comprehended in the text's examples on page 10b of "carrying/carried"; "seeing/seen"; "lover, beloved"; "leading/led." In contrast, there is the *elicitative* cause (to be explained more below). Both kinds of causalities come into play. But with regard to our need to understand OSION it is the ***elicitative*** cause which allows us to understand the fundamental character of OSION.>>

****

****

****

First of all we find that "loved by all the Gods" has become "Loved of God." <<In other words Plato allows for the nomenclature of "loved by all the Gods" as a "place-holder" (in a manner of speaking) for the first two thirds of the dialogue insofar as the multiplicity of Gods was, at that time, axiomatic. But as the analysis progresses it becomes clear that that Plato does not believe in a multiplicity of Gods and Goddesses; rather "God."
Accordingly the heading "loved by all the Gods" submits to the heading: "Loved of/by God." But this change of nomenclature still leaves us short for the understanding/defining of OSION.

In any case, Plato is saying something more than speaking of "God" in the singular. What he is projecting is amazing. It is OSION ITSELF {"Holy" but not God *per se*} which, one way or another, if you follow it closely, you will see that Plato is maintaining that even when one 'graduates' *"loved by all the Gods"* to *"Loved of/by God"* <i.e., "God" in the singular> there is something -- **OSION** -- which is on an *amazing* plateau **which is higher, so to speak, than God**. This Holy plateau is brushed by God but is not on or in It. *"Loved by all the Gods,"* is but an attribute; **SO TOO** is *"Loved of/by God"* **IS ALSO BUT AN ATTRIBUTE**. In other words, **even** with the dropping of the multiplicity of Gods and Goddesses, the single-ness of "God" **is not the final draw; rather, OSION is the draw.** The supreme entity is **OSION**. God is not the ultimate being <more like the chief Lieutenant>. **OSION** is, indeed, *"LOVED OF/BY GOD." However, "Loved of/by God"* **is but an ATTRIBUTE**. In contrast OSION *DRAWS* the love of God.
The key phrasing on pages ten and eleven is thus:
Socrates speaking: <page ten>

Then that which is dear to the Gods, Euthyphro, -- <or, if you wish, "God" in the singular> -- ***is not holy; nor is that which is HOLY <OSION> simply 'loved by/of God', as you affirm. Indeed, each way of saying it parses out as ONLY BEING AN ATTRIBUTE AND NOT THE ESSENCE OF 'OSION' <aka "HSoDaQ.">***

Euthyphro speaking:

How do you mean, Socrates?

Socrates speaking:

I mean to say that the HOLY <OSION> ***has been acknowledged by us to be loved of/by God BECAUSE IT IS HOLY; and not because it is loved.***

Again:

I mean to say that the HOLY (OSION/ HSoDaQ) ***HAS BEEN ACKNOWLEDGED BY US TO BE LOVED OF/BY GOD***

BECAUSE IT IS HOLY, AND NOT BECAUSE IT IS LOVED.

****
****
****
****
****

A NOTE ON "FAITH"

Four different words:

Hebrew: ***emunah***; abiding trust.

Greek: ***pistis***; 'the way.' Later, the Greek *pistis* picks up overtones of intellectuality.

Latin: ***fides*** <fidelity>. In some contexts, "fides" is very close to the Hebrew ***emunah***: abiding trust. But over time the deployment of ***fides*** <similar to what happened to *pistis* in Greek, but stronger> introduces to this matter an element of intellectuality. To wit:

Fides quaerens Intellectum

The Greek and Latin orientations for ***pistis*** and, with more force, ***fides***, tend towards an intellectualizing orientation for ***pistis*** and ***fides***. Such intellectualizing was the atmosphere in the late first and early second centuries in and around Alexandria, the home for many of the "Fathers of the Church." By and large the influence of the "Fathers of the Church" tended to emphasize *pistis* and *fides* as **doctrinal** words in the service of structuring the intellectual edifice of nascent Christianity.

In effect this development created a kind of "intellectual space" wherein "faith-oriented" doctrinal inventions <<The Trinity; The Divinity of Jesus; The Ascension of Yeshu; Assumption of Miriam <the mother of Yeshu> {along with Miriam being free of "Original Sin" <Itself a doctrinal invention>} and a number of other caveats also culled from thin air.>>

"Faith," it appears, has lost its way from the original Hebrew: ***emunah***: *abiding trust*.

Yes. There are in Judaism certain caveats which dance around the miraculous. But, by and large, the Jewish brush-up with 'the miraculous' parses out as the reality that Jews have survived <and often much more than surviving> for three millennia including that horrendous *SHOAH*. **THAT**, more than anything else, is truly miraculous. <<The Price? *The Six Million*>>

When it's all said and done, the only "doctrine" which matters the most is:

CHOOSE LIFE

****
English: In this language the element of intellectuality smothers over the English word "faith" in such a way that "faith" in English tends to be deployed as set of doctrines mostly generated by those 'fathers of the Church" back in Alexandria' <and elsewhere; e.g., Antioch> and continued -- at least in the Roman Church -- with caveats based on the simple fact that such and such was promulgated as being part of the Roman Church. The Roman Church, then and now, is starving from the absence of ***emunah***.
****

EMUNAH*: *abiding trust
****

The Interesting Case of *Hebrews* 11
*****
English: In our language the element of intellectuality smothers over the English word "faith" in such a way that "faith" in English is, by and large, understood as a set of doctrines mostly generated by those 'fathers of the Church back in Alexandria' and continued -- at least in the Roman Church -- with caveats based on the simple fact that such and such was promulgated as being part of the Roman Church. The Roman Church, then and now, is starving from the absence of true ***emunah***.
*****

The Book of Hebrews

The most notable feature of the "Book of Hebrews" is from the first sentence in Chapter Eleven wherein the Greek word *hupostasis* is deployed in the opening sentence. It is both a weighty word and, as well, a word which allows for multiple translations <according to the

context>. If you take the word literally, it comes forth as "standing-under." This "standing-under" brings with it an understanding which points to a *foundational* function. <<i.e., a basement of an edifice>>. Or, if you will, that in terms of which allows for predication. Something **fundamental**.
*****
In the context of the opening of *Hebrews-11* this word -- ***hupostasis*** -- can be deployed as "confidence" <which, as you can see, carries within it the root "*fides*">.
*****
Often <<indeed too often>> it is claimed by many that this document is a product of Saul/Paul. Those 'Letters' of Saul/Paul are rife with Anti-Semitism. Saul/Paul's pedigree ((a *mamzer* whose mother was not Jewish and whose Jewish father had to bribe this *mamzer* <when he achieved his majority> to foreclose any further claim to be part of the family)) was very different from that other famous *mamzer* <Yeshu> whose Mother and half-brothers and sisters welcomed him.
Yeshu was not only Jewish, but very active in Jewish affairs <albeit with some strife -- some of which was serious by virtue of the factions in Judaism at that time>.* But unlike Saul/Paul Yeshu was very comfortable with his Judaism. It was the very center of his life. He was born a Jew; raised as a Jew; faithfully involved always in Jewish matters <*halakhic* and otherwise as well> ; and died a Jew. He most certainly did not -- or even try to <indeed it would be unthinkable to Yeshu> have anything at all in generating a new religion. Period.

*. {To be sure there were rough edges -- indeed very rough edges -- between and among various Jewish factions. (((Does it not remind you of present-day Judaism???))) There were acrimonious

interchanges between the various factions. Much of this acrimony had to do with the status of the (putative) Oral Torah treasured by the Pharisaic faction. In turn Yeshu was oriented such that only the *mitsvot* of Scripture should become part of the official *HALAKHA*. From Yeshu's perspective those putative Oral Torah *halakhot* had no standing in the true *HALAKHA*. To be sure, though, there would not be any impediment against allowing those putative *halakhot* to be honored as treasured *minhaggim*.

There is another dimension here.

Yeshu often and publically castigated the members of the Pharisaic Sect (especially with regard to the plethora of Oral Torah *halakhot* and, correlatively, a plethora of Rabbinic Enactments).

In turn, the Pharisaic recipients of these castigations had no qualms about countering with castigations against Yeshu. His status as a *mamzer* <albeit by way of Jewish mother> would be thrown back to Yeshu's face in retort.

*****

And finally, and most dangerously, towards the end of the third year of his ministry, he tended to go "over-board," especially with regard to some of the most sacred dimensions of Jewish Piety. For instance -- and only two weeks prior to *THE GREAT SHABBAT* of that year -- it was recorded in his interchanges with the Pharisaic faction that Yeshu made this daring (and, arguably, ***blasphemous***):

THE FATHER AND I ARE ONE (!!!!!)

The Pharisaic members who had been jousting with Yeshu -- especially on dietary matters -- were stunned and deeply outraged by what Yeshu maintained:

THE FATHER AND I ARE ONE (!!!!!)

At this point the Pharisaic members were outraged. Spontaneously they picked up rocks and stones and threw them at Yeshu. Yeshu had to retreat to a forest just above the knoll where all this happened.*

*. ((Yeshu -- always argumentative -- had been affected deeply by having been chosen as the center piece <along with the young El'azar ben Hurcanus> of a Plan hatched by the High Priest which, in theory, would put both Yeshu and El'azar *on top of a mountain!* <so to speak>.

Now everybody has some degree of narcissism. But Yeshu -- ever doted upon by his mother even when Yeshu was thirty years old -- was "over-the-top" in his narcissism. Yes. El'azar was also affected as well. But with this difference. El'azar was excited. Yeshu had no bounds. In other words, Yeshu had become dangerous without really understanding that he had become dangerous <to himself and to others>. Yeshu's exclamation on that day ----- the day when Yeshu maintained that:

THE FATHER AND I ARE ONE (!!!!!)

))

****

****

Continuing on:

Except for the status of ***hupostasis*** <best understood <<< ONLY IN THIS CONTEXT>>> as "confidence"> the rest of *Hebrews* – Eleven (and for that matter the whole document) is not all that remarkable. To wit and staccatically :

i). Again:

"***hupostasis***/confidence." Just as a word, it already carries weight. in particular it joins with "***emunah"*** as words which largely stand, just by themselves, not needing those words (which we have already reviewed) which shunts us over to the ***intellectual*** plane. And that is good.

ii). Saul/Paul did not generate neither *Hebrews Eleven* nor *Hebrews* as a whole. *There is no Anit-Semitism in* **this** *production.* Paul, however, can hardly write a single paragraph without promulgating a direct or indirect slur on "The Jews."

iii). The largest dimension of *Hebrews* is a cataloguing of the history of the world and, more germane, the history of the Jewish People <i.e. prior to the time of Yeshu>. This is not a smear job at all. On the contrary this review of Jewish History is calculated to show ((i.e., ***ATTEMPT*** to show)) THAT THE GREAT CHAPTERS OF THE Jewish People can be understood as gliding into the ministry and life of Yeshu.

The problem of course is that this attempt at melding is an attempt which cannot support itself. Yeshu was not a "goody/goody." You know that; I know that. But even if he were a "goody/goody" it would not be enough.

Indeed "goody/goody" is not the appropriate accounting of the Jewish People in History. And, *a fortiori* "goody/goody" does not successfully characterize what Yeshu was about.

*****

Let's bring this chapter to a close. A Square is not a Circle and visa/visa. The reality is that Yeshu had no

sense at all about starting an other religion. Yeshu was born a Jew; lived his whole life as a Jew; and died as a Jew.
Yes. There were some Jews <who had never been in the company of Yeshu in the flesh> who attempted to graduate the figure of Yeshu as a kind of cult figure. There are some strained dimensions of such in the early redactions of what would become the Gospel of Matthew. But these Jewish enthusiasts who attempted such were not at all involved in launching a new religion. And that's all.
The birthing of Christianity is a function of Saul/ Paul's "Letters" <<rife with Anti-Semitism>>. Saul/ Paul created out of whole-cloth a figure larger than life; a figure of what Saul/Paul's dreams of his own putative greatness. Saul/Paul created a fictional figure; a figure created in the image and likeness of Saul/Paul's narcissism.
As I have said above, had Yeshu himself had ever come across Saul/Paul Yeshu would have viciously castigated Saul/Paul as being a first-rate anti-Semitic fraud.
*****
Other than that, *The Book of Hebrews* is slim pickings. In other words, this document belongs to a sparse -- and largely puerile -- dream that, somewhere somehow, there can be some sort of "arrangement" whereby the manufactured figure of Yeshu in the New Testament can also function as the true Yeshu who was born a Jew; lived as a Jew; and died as a Jew.
The simple reality is that the New Testament created a "Yeshu" who never existed.
****
****
****
****
****

When Moses ascended to the (Heavenly) *Heights he found the Holy One, blessed be He, as He was sitting and attaching crowns to some of the letters* (and adding *tagin* to certain letters). *Moses said to His face:* "Who is holding you back (from giving the Torah as it is)*? Hashem replied to him:* "There is a man who is destined to exist at the end of many generations ------- Aqiba ben Yosef is his name; he will expound upon each and every matter <u>HEAPS UPON HEAPS OF *HALAKHOT*.</u>"

Moses addressed the face of Hashem: "Master of the Universe, show him to me!" *Hashem said to him:* "Turn around" (he, <Moses> found himself in Aqiba's class)*. Moses went and sat at the end of eight rows of students. But he* (Moses <who received the Law from Sinai) *did not understand what they were saying. Moses' strength ebbed. Once they reached a certain matter which was puzzling. Aqiba's students asked him:* "from what source do you know this? *Aqiba replied* (cavalierly): "It is a *halakha* transmitted from the mouth of Moses at Sinai."

Moses' mind was relieved. He returned and came before the Holy One, blessed be He. Moses said to His face:

"YOU HAVE SOMEONE LIKE THIS AND YOU GIVE THE TORAH TRHOUGH ME!!??"

Hashem said to him: "SHUSH! Thus has it arisen in the thoughts before Me."

Moses said to His face:

"Master of the Universe, You have shown me his Torah; now show me his reward."

"TURN AROUND."

Moses turned around and saw that the people were weighing the flesh from [Aqiba's body] *in the meat market.*

Moses said before Hashem:

"MASTER OF THE UNIVERSE"!!! Such is his Torah and THIS is reward???
Hashem replied:
"QUIET!!!! SUCH IS MY DECREE.

*****   *****   *****

****
****
****

When this or that existing Theology interferes with the natural meaning of Scripture, it only means that the Theology at issue is defective. One only needs to say "Maimonides" to recognize that (as an example) in *The Guide for the Perplexed* our Jewish Scripture is accessed largely through the Aristotelian prism <quite apart from the Hebrew <or Aramaic> text itself>. Such is the paradigmatic example by which -- generation unto generation -- a "slanting" <in this case, Aristotelian> of our Scripture is put forth in accordance with this or that "slanting" involved. Such is the stain on Judaism which remains with us now.
Nor has Judaism freed Itself from those Hellenic <and other> strictures over the centuries.

Printed in the United States
By Bookmasters